The Modern Bartender

Jason Jelicich

HOSPITALITY
PRESS
MELBOURNE

Hospitality Press Pty Ltd
38 Riddell Parade
PO Box 426
Elsternwick Victoria 3185
Australia
Telephone (+61 3) 9528 5021 Fax (+61 3) 9528 2645
Email hosppress@access.net.au

The Modern Bartender
First published 2001

National Library of Australia
Cataloguing-in-publication data:

Jelicich, Jason, 1970–.

   The modern bartender.
   includes index.
   ISBN 1 86250 493 8.

   1. Bartenders. 2. Bartending – Handbooks, manuals, etc. I. Title.

641.874

Edited by Neil Conning & Associates
Designed by Lauren Statham (Alice Graphics)
Front cover shows bartenders Craig Widdicombe and Sarah Wemberley at
the Iguana Bar, Sydney
Cover photograph by Danielle Lyonne
Printed in Malayasia
Published by Hospitality Press Pty Ltd (ABN 69 935 151 798)

Foreword

In *The Modern Bartender*, Jason Jelicich has delivered a book that, in the hospitality industry, is the first of its kind. I am sure it will be embraced by all bartenders in the way that it deserves. Jason has long been considered one of the most respected and innovative thinkers in our industry and his years of experience shine through in this detailed and informative read.

As a bartender, trainer, consultant, adviser and figurehead, Jason has been a significant part of the lift in standards that has occurred over the last couple of years in Australia. His Speedpour training courses are a step above and beyond anything anyone else is doing at present and it is inspiring to see someone so passionate about their trade focus on sharing their wealth of knowledge with other like-minded professionals.

From the novice to the expert, anyone who reads *The Modern Bartender* will take something away from it. Jason leaves no stone unturned in providing hints on service, efficiency and communication in a manner that is detailed, up-to-date and easy to follow. As a good friend and colleague, I have no hesitation in saying that this is a must for every bar and every bartender serious about improving their skills.

Naren Young
Editor, *Australian Bartender*

Dedicated to those who work behind a bar and
dare to regard themselves as professionals

Acknowledgements

There are many people I would like to acknowledge for their part in bringing this book to fruition. Firstly, I would like to thank my wife Helen for believing in me and encouraging me as I left a comfy corporate job in pursuit of a passion. Secondly I would like to thank my publisher who took a punt on the idea. I would also like to thank John Halmarick from United Distillers and Vintners, who has backed me when I needed it most.

I would also like to acknowledge the assistance of the following people: photographer, Danielle Lyonne, who took charge of the photography and offered me her expertise and enthusiasm at a fraction of its market value; editor, Neil Conning, who helped me look at the finer detail and became quite a textbook bartender in the process; designer, Lauren Statham, who made everything fit together harmoniously; good friend and artist, Matthew Dale, for his advice and illustrations along the way; Alf de Hombre, whose creative influence has motivated and guided me from day one.

A special thank you to Ulysses at Café Iguana as well as the guys at Bar Cleveland, The Cave Nightclub and the Embassy Nightclub, for being so accommodating to me over all these years.

Thanks also to all the bar owners, bar managers, bartenders and glassies from around Australia and the world, who have taught me better ways of doing the job and who have constantly provided me with their different perspectives on a job we all love – bartending.

Contents

1

Introduction

The modern bartender is a new breed of hospitality professional, dedicated to meeting the needs of the customer.

The hospitality industry has seen dramatic growth over the past 10 years, with the traditional pub now giving way to a new generation of speed service bars. This has forced major changes to the bartender's workplace, with today's bartenders expected to be able to work more quickly and effectively than their predecessors.

To keep up with the changes in the industry, bartenders must be quick to adapt to new challenges. Speed service techniques and multiple drink mixing are now essential skills to master in order to make headway in this increasingly competitive industry. Bartenders must be faster, more knowledgeable and more customer-focused than ever before.

Today's bartender considers the optimum level of customer service as the number one priority. He or she is proactive, shows initiative and does not hesitate to add value to the customers' service experience. Efficient drink preparation skills are also practised to keep pace with demand and ensuring that all drinks being prepared are to the customers' satisfaction.

The Modern Bartender focuses on these skill sets, including money handling, customer interaction and drink preparation skills, providing a valuable reference source for busy bars and fledgling bartenders alike. The book aims to provide up-to-date and relevant information on the trade, giving readers an edge in today's rapidly changing industry.

Products sold over the bar are explained, and readers are given detailed lists of fruit, juices and condiments that turn an average bar into an excellent one. The chapter on customer service looks at how a bartender can best utilise communication skills to manage a busy bar. Examples indicate the type of language that may be used to optimise service. The chapter on preparing drinks covers everything from pouring beer and spirits to opening wine and bottled beer, with detailed instructions, clear pictures and handy tips.

The topic of multiple drink mixing reveals the secrets of large order preparation, with a strong focus on efficiency. Cocktails are grouped into categories and simple guidelines are given for mixing them from scratch. The recipes include commonly ordered cocktails as well as specialities.

Take your time to learn. Practise and perfect the skills and knowledge contained within this book. Constantly challenge yourself to improve areas of your service and become a 'professional' in the process.

The process of learning

Development of skill sets such as bartending can be split into four stages.

Stage 1

Unconscious incompetence
(You don't know what you don't know)

This is the starting point – before you even have the notion of learning bartending. When you become aware of your lack of competence, you move to Stage 2.

Awareness

Stage 2

Conscious incompetence

(You know what you don't know)

You begin to entertain the notion of bartending but still do not know how to do it. You are aware that you are incompetent (in that particular skill) and through training you are able to reach Stage 3.

Training

Stage 3

Conscious competence

(You know what you know)

You learn the basics or attend a bar college and become proficient. Through practice you are able to move to Stage 4.

Practice

Stage 4

Unconscious competence

(The knowledge/skill is second nature)

Once you have had a chance to practise and apply the skills, they can be completed with little conscious thought. This is the stage where the necessary skills are completely mastered.

2

The modern bartender

The modern bartender needs both good communication skills and efficient bar service skills.

The modern bartender plays an important social role in the community, helping to balance the work and stress of modern day society with a good measure of fun and excitement. It could be said that the primary role the bartender plays is that of a social facilitator – someone whose outgoing personality and positive demeanor energises his or her clientele and promotes good times.

Skilled drink preparation, although essential to practise and perfect, plays more of a secondary function in the bar room environment with alcoholic beverages acting as social lubricants – helping people to relax and unwind after a hard day at work.

Truly great bartenders understand this and focus their attention on balancing effective over-the-bar communication with solid drink preparation skills – leaving their customers with a lasting positive impression of their service as a result.

Other qualities that are essential to the modern bartender include:

Attitude

There is no room for arrogance in a bar. If a bartender has trouble with other staff members or customers, he or she should be counselled as soon as possible. Work should be fun, and a bartender with a bad mood should be asked to leave it at the door.

People need to work as a team in a bar to be productive and this becomes unsettled when someone is not participating or 'putting in'. A bartender should have a positive disposition whenever on duty.

Arrogance towards customers is not acceptable. Bar staff who talk back or are off-hand with customers should be counselled immediately and not allowed to serve customers until they have cooled down.

Grooming

Looking professional is important. Male bartenders should be cleanly shaven or have facial hair trimmed. Long hair should be pulled back from the face. Female bartenders should not wear too much makeup and should wear only basic jewellery.

Clothing should be appropriate for the venue, and if there is a staff uniform it should be kept clean and unwrinkled. If no staff uniform is required, a bartender should find out what the other bartenders wear and wear something similar. It is important that staff look their best. When people look good they feel better and often perform better due to an increased level of confidence.

Preparation

Preparation is the key to success. A bartender should be 'set for success' by having everything on hand that will be needed during the shift.

When preparing a bar for a shift, a bartender needs to think of anything that may inhibit service to customers. Running out of things is sometimes unavoidable, but to run out of too many things is unacceptable. Preparation is important for the smooth running of a busy bar. Everything should be clean, fresh and full at the start of the shift, with backup supplies close at hand.

Bartenders should always have on hand some necessary basic items. A pen, for example, is essential for running tabs and keeping records. A cigarette lighter is sometimes needed, as lighting cigarettes is sometimes part of a bartender's repertoire. Bartenders should also bring their own bottle opener and/or waiter's friend.

Basic items

▼ Pen
▼ Cigarette lighter
▼ Bottle opener

Prioritisation

In a busy bar it is important to prioritise the work at hand. This sorts out the jobs that should be done immediately from those that are not as urgent. Service to customers is a bartender's number one objective. For example, if a bartender polishing glasses notices someone is waiting for a drink, they would leave the glasses until later and serve the customer immediately. Customer service should come before jobs such as washing glasses, restocking fruit, and counting change.

An exception to this is when something is about to run out. The bartender may need to tell the customer, 'I won't be long,' and then quickly replenish the stock before serving.

A bartender's key priorities

1 **Servers** – Serve cocktail servers or waiters first. They represent customers who are already waiting.
2 **Bar patrons** – Acknowledge bar patrons immediately, and serve them in order of arrival at the bar.
3 **Cleaning** – Clean up progressively. Wipe the surfaces and clear the bar of glasses and ashtrays while taking orders.
4 **Restocking** – Constantly check and replenish stock before things run out.

Multi-tasking

Multi-tasking involves doing more than one thing at a time. Combining jobs is essential behind the bar, and a bartender should endeavour to complete as many tasks as possible, either at the same time or in quick succession.

For example, when a bartender is serving a customer, he or she should automatically clean the area around the customer – removing dirty glasses and wiping the bar. By doing this, the bartender keeps the bar-top clean throughout the shift, as well as providing good service to the customers.

> By doing more than one thing at a time, a bartender is able to work more efficiently and stay in control of a busy bar.

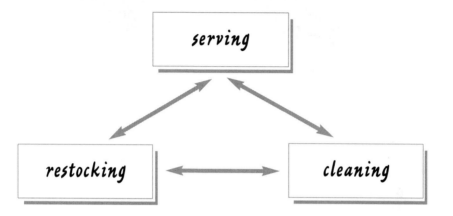

Teamwork

Hospitality is a team business, and when one member of the team is not functioning properly it can put a strain on the whole operation. Bartenders should be prepared to work in a team when appropriate, and should utilise and assist the people around them to achieve better results.

For example, if an order is taken over the bar for several mixed drinks and a beer and the bartender decides to complete it unassisted, this might take longer than possible to prepare, while other staff stand idle. If, on the other hand, he or she calls the beers to another staff member to fetch while preparing the mixed drinks, time is saved and teamwork is promoted.

From taking orders to collecting money and all jobs in between, tasks should be delegated and shared by the team, the common goal being a high level of service to customers.

Job roles

Good communication skills and an enthusiastic outlook are necessary traits in the hospitality industry. This applies to those planning a career in the hospitality industry as well as to casual workers.

> Customer communication is discussed in Chapter 8, Customer Service.

As bar work is at the 'front line', bartenders are expected to be confident in dealings with customers as well as familiar with the products and bar layout.

Hospitality training colleges are helpful in acquiring knowledge, but there is no substitute for on-the-job training. The following is an example of a possible career path progression through the bar.

Career path progression

Bar useful/glassy

Responsibilities can include collecting/washing/replenishing glassware, and general front-of-house maintenance such as cleaning tables and changing ashtrays. The bar useful does not normally have customer service contact behind the bar.

Assistant bartender/bar-back

Responsibilities can include replenishing stock and behind-the-bar maintenance such as cleaning the bar-top and taking rubbish out. The bar-back assists the bartender by taking drink orders and money and fetching stock. The bar-back may also sometimes work in the service well when the bartender is taking a break.

Bartender

Responsibilities can include taking drink orders from customers, mixing cocktails, delegating of work to bar-backs and bar-usefuls, and bar area maintenance. The bartender is also responsible for the takings at the end of the shift.

Bar supervisor/team leader

Responsibilities can include the profitability of the bar during the shift, staff breaks, customer complaints during the shift and the totalling of takings. The bar supervisor is also responsible for induction and training during the shift.

Bar manager

Responsibilities can include overall profitability of the bar, staff rostering, organisation of product promotions, major bar maintenance, and coordination of training. The bar manager reports to the general manager.

CHAPTER 3

Serving alcohol

Bartenders must be familiar with liquor laws and rules for responsible service of alcohol.

Alcohol and the law

Today's bartenders work in an industry that is heavily regulated compared to the era of their predecessors. With this in mind it is imperative that bartenders become familiar with the laws that impact upon them and their workplaces.

Although the laws and regulations governing licensed premises vary, they are common in many respects. For example, it is illegal in all states and territories to serve alcohol to minors (people under 18 years old) or to a customer who is in a state of intoxication.

Intoxication

Intoxication due to alcohol consumption causes notable changes in behaviour. All states and territories have clear guidelines regarding the service of alcohol to customers who are in a state of intoxication, and fines may apply. Allowing intoxicated people continued access to alcohol is not only against the law, but it is also bad for business, as it can annoy and endanger customers and staff.

Signs of intoxication

▼ A notable change in behaviour (especially anti-social or inappropriate behavior)
▼ Slurring of, or mistakes in speech
▼ Clumsiness, knocking things over or fumbling with change
▼ Loss of coordination (swaggering, swaying)
▼ Confusion, inability to understand, hear or respond

Bartenders play a key role in dealing with intoxicated people on the premises. It pays to be proactive in preventing intoxication to avoid problems and to keep other customers safe and happy.

Strategies to prevent intoxication

- ▼ Train staff to recognise signs of intoxication how to deal with intoxicated customers
- ▼ Promote low-alcohol drinks (e.g. light beer, low-alcohol cocktails)
- ▼ Provide food
- ▼ Display house policies
- ▼ Avoid irresponsible liquor promotions (e.g. two drinks for the price of one)
- ▼ Provide security where appropriate
- ▼ Inform customers and staff of their legal obligations

One of the hardest things for a bartender to do is to cease liquor service to ('cut off') a regular customer. Some bartenders find it difficult to stand their ground or to tackle the issue of intoxication with customers.

The recommended strategy is to intervene early and explain the bar's house policy as it applies to intoxication. It is also the responsibility of the bartender to inform the manager and security as well as other relevant staff.

Refusal of service

- ▼ Inform the manager and other staff of the intention to refuse service
- ▼ Firmly but politely refuse service and explain the law
- ▼ Seek assistance from the intoxicated person's friends
- ▼ Do not engage in arguments, and lower rather than raise your voice
- ▼ Ensure a consistent standard of service to all patrons

Minors

An important aspect of a bartender's job role is to avoid serving under-age drinkers. There are substantial fines for serving or supplying alcohol to minors (people under 18), so adequate precautions are necessary when suspicions are aroused.

What to look for

- ▼ Signs of immaturity (nervousness, lack of eye contact)
- ▼ Knowledge of drinks (often inadequate)
- ▼ Over-confident behaviour (e.g. showing off on arrival)
- ▼ Groups of young people during school holidays

Bartenders should not assume that just because there is security at the door that no one under-age has managed to enter the premises.

Verifying age and identity

▼ Look and feel for bumps or rough edges on ID card

▼ Check hologram and/or seal

▼ Check date of birth

▼ Ask for secondary ID

▼ Ask questions (e.g. age next birthday, address details)

It is not enough simply to check the date of birth and count back 18 years. The bartender should check to see if the ID is genuine.

Alcohol and driving

Alcohol-related injuries and fatalities are of major concern for governments. Since the introduction of a PCA (prescribed concentration of alcohol in the blood) in 1968 there have been many campaigns to curb the problem. The national blood alcohol limit is 0.05, which means 0.05 grams of alcohol to 100 mL of blood.

Staff on licensed premises must be aware of their duty of care for their patrons, ensuring that they are able to offer everything from advice on standard drinks to safer alternatives to driving if the need arises.

Alternatives to driving

▼ Calling a cab for the customer

▼ Calling a friend or relative to pick them up

▼ Suggesting a sober friend drives them home

▼ Advising on public transport times or courtesy buses

▼ Offering accommodation

Standard drinks

An important part of regulation of the use of alcohol with regard to drink driving has been the introduction and promotion of standard drinks labelling. By law, all pre-packed alcoholic products must state on the label how many standard drinks they contain, assisting the consumer to make an informed decision on how much they are able to drink (if any) when driving.

A 'standard drink' is an alcoholic drink that contains 12.5 mL of ethyl alcohol. The table below gives approximate serving sizes for the major liquor categories.

Serving sizes for standard drinks

Alcoholic beverage	Approximate percentage – alcohol by volume	Serving size per standard drink
Spirits	40	30 mL
Fortified wine (e.g. port)	20	60 mL
Wine	12	120 mL
Full-strength beer	4–5	285 mL
Light beer	2–3	425 mL

To remain under the 0.05 PCA the following guidelines are recommended:

Males: Two standard drinks the first hour and a maximum of one each hour thereafter

Females: One standard drink the first hour and a maximum of one each hour thereafter

It is illegal to be *on* the 0.05 limit.

Incident book

An incident book is used to record events or incidents that relate to service of alcohol. It provides a log of actions taken by staff to prevent minors and intoxicated people being on the premises, as well as incidents involving anti-social behaviour. The incident book may be used as evidence in a licensing court. (To be admissible as evidence the incident book must be free from gaps or spaces, which may allow information to be added long after the event.)

Bartenders are required to record the following information after refusing service or asking a patron to leave the premises:

▼ Time and date of incident
▼ Circumstances/situation
▼ Description of person and name if known
▼ Action taken
▼ Signature of staff and/or manager

4

Money handling

The modern bartender must be part mixologist and part mathematician.

The careful and accurate handling of money is imperative in all retail sales jobs, and bars are no exception.

Bars are unlike other retailers in that the conditions in which the money is handled are often noisy, dark and wet, increasing opportunities for mistakes to occur. The pace at which money is handled is often very fast, and many sales are for small, low-priced items that are quickly prepared. If a bartender is not vigilant, mistakes may be made with change. Bartenders need to account for discrepancies in their takings at the end of a shift, and action is necessary if discrepancies persist.

The register

The register (till) is used for management of stock and money. It is important for a bartender to use the register quickly, confidently and accurately in order to perform transactions in the minimum possible time.

Most bar registers have buttons programmed for the various products. These are displayed on the face of the register and often colour-coded for easy identification. It pays for the bartender to become familiar with the positioning of the buttons on the face before operating the register. Each different register set-up will take a couple of hours to get used to. Some new register systems use computer technology including touch screens to access products and prices.

Bartenders should regard money in the till as the outcome of their work, and like their work, keep it tidy and organised.

Codes vary, but here are some functions that are found on most bar registers.

NS	No sale (opens till drawer)
VOID	Error correction (clears last transaction)
RCT COPY	Prints receipt for last transaction
CL	Clear (clears screen only)
ST	Subtotal (does not open drawer)
RCT Feed	Feeds receipt or printer paper through
PLU	Price look-up
TOT	Total (opens drawer)
JNL Feed	Feeds journal paper through

Electronic registers often have a separate printer for receipts.

16

Common register terms

Receipt A paper record of the transaction intended for the customer. It can also be used to record an over-ring (refer below).

Journal A paper record of register transactions, including no sales, and management functions. The business must keep the journal roll for tax purposes.

Over-ring (O/R) A mistake on the register when an amount has been entered accidentally but no money has gone in the drawer. A copy of the transaction is often printed and the manager adjusts the records either during or at the end of the shift.

X-read A management function that gives a progress total of transactions, but does not reset the register. This read can be used to check a register's total during a shift but it is most often used to ensure the right amount of money is taken before a Z-Read.

Z-read A management function that gives a total of all the shift's transactions, and resets the register back to zero.

Floats

Floats are generally made up of bundles of notes and bags or tubes of coins for ease of counting, and a bartender must be familiar with how much each contains in order to count it quickly and accurately.

Standard bundles of notes and bags or tubes of coins as they come from the bank are listed in the table below.

Denominations	Units	Total ($)
$100	10	1,000
$50	10	500
$20	10	200
$10	10	100
$5	10	50
$2	25	50
$1	20	20
50¢	20	10
20¢	50	10 (bag) 4 (tube)
10¢	100	10 (bag) 4 (tube)

Common float totals are usually somewhere between $200 and $500 but they can go as high as $1,000, depending on how long the shift runs for and how busy it is expected to be.

Floats are comprised of coinage and small denominations of notes to make up the total. There is no need for large notes such as $50 or $100 as they do not assist the bartender in making change.

If a bartender receives a float and is told by the manager that it contains $200, the amount received should be checked upon receipt. If the float is short $50 and the manager has counted incorrectly, the bartender's receipts will appear to be down at the end of the shift.

A typical float of $500

When counting the float, it is common practice to draw up a chart, and to note each denomination as it is counted. This helps keep track of how much money has been counted up to that point in the case of a distraction. It also serves as guide to help the bartender double-check the denominations if the need arises (e.g. if the amount counted is 'under' or 'over' the expected total).

Denomination	Units	Total ($)	Checked
$20	1	20	✔
$10	8	80	✔
$5	20	100	✔
$2	50	100	✔
$1	100	100	✔
50¢	100	50	✔
20¢	200	40	✔
10¢	100	10	✔
		Total $500	✔

Till drawer layout

After the float has been counted, the money is arranged in the till drawer in the most convenient way for access. Notes and coins should be in order from largest to smallest, enabling the till user to 'count up' change for a customer in an ordered fashion.

There are several ways of laying out a till, but here are two popular methods:

The first way starts with $50 notes from the top right across to $5 notes on the top left. The $2 coins begin on the bottom left and denominations range to the smaller demoninations on the bottom right.

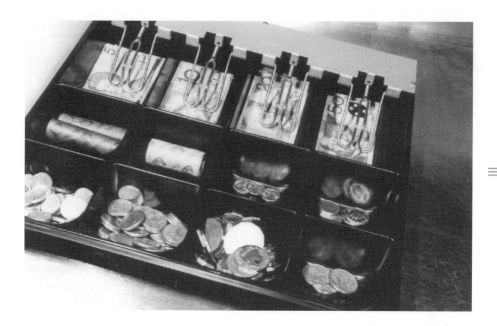

The second way is basically the opposite, with $50 notes starting at the top left, and finishing up with small coins on the bottom left. Hundred dollar notes are often placed under the till drawer to avoid giving them out accidentally.

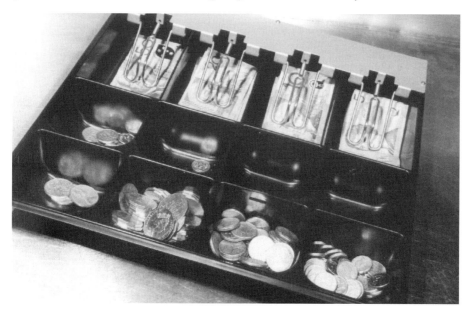

Making change

A bartender is constantly counting money during the course of a shift and must be alert in order to avoid making mistakes. One way to ensure the bartender stays thinking is through the process of 'counting up'. Counting up involves 'rounding' up the change by starting with the small coins and moving up to the larger coins and notes.

Example of 'counting up'

Sale totals $13.40

Customer gives $20

- ▼ Bartender counts up 60¢ (to make $14.00)
- ▼ Then $1 (to make $15.00)
- ▼ Then $5 (to make $20)

Change can also be calculated using the subtotal function or denomination keys ($5, $10, $20).

Many registers have preset keys for money tendered, eliminating the need for calculation by the bartender.

A cash transaction step by step

- ▼ Enter transaction on register and press 'subtotal' (if not known)
- ▼ Take money from customer
- ▼ Enter the amount of money handed over followed by total/cash (this will calculate the change amount)
- ▼ Place all notes in the till the same way (some bartenders leave notes on top of drawer until change is counted – in case of confusion)
- ▼ Count up the change starting from the smaller coins to the larger notes
- ▼ Place change on a change plate and position in front of customer or in customer's hand, stating change amount to customer ('That's $4.50 change, thanks.')

Efficiency tip

Often it is convenient to take money from more than one customer at a time. This is especially relevant when the bartender has combined an order and has to move more than a few steps to get back to the register. There is no point making two trips to the register if it can be done in a single trip.

Electronic payment

Most bars offer electronic funds transfer (EFTPOS) and credit card facilities. The operation of the equipment is simple, with the machine guiding the user through the necessary steps. The steps are as follows:

▼ Enter transaction on register and press 'subtotal'
▼ Take card and swipe through machine
▼ Ask customer to enter pin number and press OK (if EFTPOS)
▼ Enter register total and press ENTER or OK
▼ Ask customer about money out (if EFTPOS)
▼ Customer to sign (if credit card)
▼ Totalise register
▼ Customer receives copy and original is kept in register

CHAPTER 5

The modern bar

The modern bar is designed with ease of service in mind.

As the hospitality industry progresses, bars are being renovated, including new features, improving both customer comfort and efficiency.

The modern bar is a far cry from its traditional ancestor, the public or local bar, with smart design and layout allowing the bartender to be more productive. Today's bar tends to have a larger ice well to cater for the increasing proportion of mixed drink orders. Beer taps have been designed with single stems and smaller drip drays to save valuable space.

Fridge space has increased to hold and display the growing range of bottled beers and pre-mixed beverages.

Other changes include increased traffic area behind the bar to assist bartender movement and preparation of drinks. Larger and more accessible sinks and glasswashers are also a feature of modern bars.

Bar sections

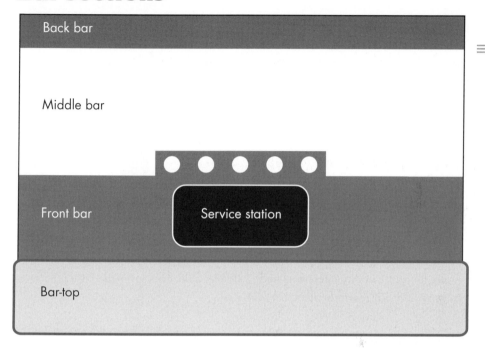

The bar-top

The main function the bar-top performs is that of a counter, over which beverages are served. But there are also other ways in which the bar-top is used: as a spot to relax, a place to survey the crowd, or a place to sit and wait for company.

The bar-top is the main place where the bartender interacts with customers, and it should represent all that the bar is trying to project – cleanliness, comfort and good organisation. It should be kept clean and well-organised to maintain a professional image. This simply involves wiping the bar, cleaning ashtrays and clearing dirty glasses.

The front bar

The front bar is where the bartender should spend most time, either mixing at the service station or serving customers over the bar-top. The organisation of the front bar is important for efficiency.

Many front bars are made of stainless steel, incorporating into them the ice wells, sinks and other major fittings. In some bars it may be hard to make space on the front bar because of poor design or outmoded fittings, so a bartender must think carefully about what to 'bring forward' (from the back bar) and what to 'leave behind'. The front bar generally houses the bar's most commonly used glassware, products and equipment.

The service station

The service station is an important part of the front bar. This is where the bartender prepares mixed drinks and cocktails. Large bars may have a number of service stations, with each servicing a section of the bar. Smaller venues may have only one service station, with the bartender performing a number of tasks from it, e.g. making coffees, taking orders for the restaurant, and serving customers.

The middle bar/traffic area

The middle bar is the space between the front bar and the back bar in which the bar team works. A bar must have good traffic flow for the staff to be able to move around each other easily and quickly. Bars with insufficient room to move behind the bar do not operate efficiently. If the middle bar is too big, then the back bar equipment and products might be too far away. A good amount of space to have behind a bar is generally the width of three people standing side by side. This gives the bartender room to move and still reach the back bar with ease.

The back bar

The back bar is the area where the majority of the bar's products are generally displayed, including spirits, liqueurs and bottled beers. It is also often used as the point-of-sale area for popular and new products.

The back bar is often split into two sections, with fridges at the bottom and shelving at the top. The fridges are stocked with bottled beers, etc. faced out (labels facing towards the customer) to assist in the selling process. The shelving above provides space for premium spirits and liqueurs to be displayed. Shelving and bottles should be cleaned and polished regularly.

Bar dynamics

The dynamics of a bar are similar regardless of its shape or size. There is always a service area where the bartender stands to prepare drinks and a back bar used to store and display products. The bartender should ideally be centred at the service area (station) and should ideally not have to move more than one or two steps to complete drinks.

The bartender should be using peripheral vision and also be able to easily see the bar service area for which he or she is responsible. Obstacles to vision such as fixtures are likely to affect over-the-bar communication and customer service. A bartender should not work from the back bar, because it is difficult to keep an eye on new customers coming to the bar.

> If a bartender has to move more than a few steps to complete drinks, thought should be given to relocating the items required.

Efficiency tip

In large bars a smart way for a bartender to work is to 'call' for a product or piece of equipment to be brought by a colleague, used on the front bar, then returned. By using the team and not having to leave the service station, the bartender is able to keep an eye on what is happening while mixing the drinks, therefore promoting efficiency.

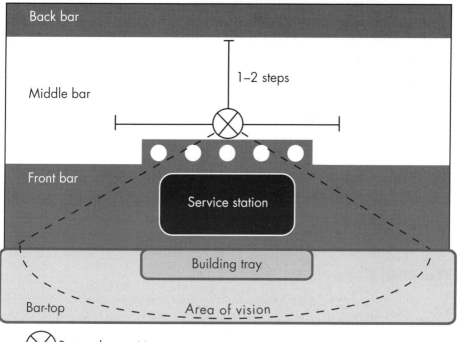

Back bar

Middle bar

1–2 steps

Front bar

Service station

Building tray

Bar-top   Area of vision

 Bartender position

Fixed equipment

The design of bar fixtures can contribute greatly towards bar efficiency. For example, if the ice well is too small or the bench space is insufficient, efficiency will be jeopardised.

Bar designs are moving away from the standard draught beer bar layouts towards a more American style, with increased focus on mixed drinks and cocktails – sometimes even omitting beer taps completely. Fixed equipment in most bars includes the following:

Ice well

Deep and with drainage, the ice well is moulded in stainless steel and should hold enough ice to service busy periods. The ice well forms the centre of the service station

Speed rack

Either built into the bar or clipped on, the speed rack provides fast, easy access to popular spirits and liqueurs. It should be made from stainless steel and be lined with cloth or sponge to provide cushioning when replacing bottles.

Building tray

The building tray is a long flat surface at the service station on which the bartender prepares mixed drinks. It can either be built into the design of the bar or attached to an existing bar. They are often made of stainless steel, but sometimes simply consist of a rubber mat.

Sink

A large stainless steel sink is important for all bars. The sink should be in a central position in the bar allowing access from all service stations. Where there are a number of service stations, additional sinks may be included in the design to minimise bartender movement.

Glasswasher

Glasswashers should be positioned near an entrance to the bar, allowing staff quick access from outside the bar. The space above the glasswasher should be reserved for dirty glass racks, of which there are usually two or three.

Fridges

Fridges provide a display area for packaged products and should ideally be positioned at the back of the bar, allowing customers to view their contents. They usually feature see-though doors, along with lights and large, convenient handles.

Post-mix machine

The post-mix gun is the space-efficient cousin of the older-style counter-top post-mix unit. Fitted with a long hose, this unit is flexible, even fun to use, when adding sodas to drinks. A service station may feature two post-mix guns (one on each side) to allow access for two bartenders.

Beer taps

In the traditional bar, beer taps take up a large proportion of available front bar space. Beer font designs are becoming more space-efficient, with multiple fonts combined into the one stem. This allows more space on the front bar for other purposes.

Spirit dispensers

Electronic spirit dispensers are used in many bars, often in banks of four to six bottles. These dispense drinks efficiently and accurately.

Bar equipment

Bars are expected to offer a wide variety of beverages to a growing number of educated palates and in order to the achieve this the following equipment is essential:

Ice blender

A blender is essential piece of equipment. Its main function is to blend fruit and ice with other ingredients. A plastic food processor is not suitable for this use and will not create a smooth consistency. A stainless steel blender with a sturdy motor is a must.

Cocktail shaker – standard/Boston/ American

A good quality shaker is essential. The shaker is made from stainless steel and ideally includes a mixing glass (American shaker). Both the Boston and standard shakers have three parts – a tin base, an inbuilt strainer and a lid. The two-part American shaker is commonly used in cocktail bars, and requires a separate strainer.

Cocktail strainer

Known as a Hawthorne strainer, this item is made of stainless steel and features a wire coil. It is used to strain the ice out of cocktails and mixed drinks.

Mixing spoon

This is a long-handled spoon with a twisted shaft and a flat muddler end. The 'muddler' is used to crush sugar in certain drinks while the mixing spoon is used to stir cocktails in the mixing glass. The spoon is also sometimes used to layer drinks.

Muddling stick

Increasingly common in the modern bar, this heavy-duty pestle is used to muddle (crush) sugar and fruit together. It is most commonly used for the Caipiroska (see Cocktail Recipes).

Ice scoop

A large ice scoop is essential for efficient mixing. Being able to put more ice in each scoop means preparation of faster drinks. The base of a shaker can be used as an ice scoop.

Wine opener

Commonly called a 'waiter's friend', this item is essential for opening bottles of wine. There is an attachment for opening beer bottles, but it is not the best tool for this task.

> Knife
> Lever
> Corkscrew

Bottle opener

A long-handled speed opener is ideal for busy bars where large numbers of bottles require opening.

Garnish tray

A garnish tray is used to store a variety of prepared garnishes and keeps them fresh and handy. It ideally should have a number of compartments for different fruits and garnishes. For hygiene purposes, tongs should ideally be used for handling fruit garnishes.

Cutting board and fruit knife

A good-sized cutting board should be made of non-absorbent materials such as polythene. Wood is not recommended.

A sharp fruit knife is needed to cut garnishes accurately to size. A small serrated knife is best for this purpose.

Fruit chaneller

A fruit chaneller is designed to prepare 'twists' of peel for cocktails, and is often combined with a zester, which is used to grate the rind.

Spirit measures (jiggers)

15 mL and 30 mL measures are required to measure ingredients accurately for mixed drinks and cocktails. They must be approved by the National Standards Commission, which is signified by a small set of scales imprinted on the unit.

Free-pourers

Free-pourers should be fitted to bottles of commonly used alcoholic ingredients behind the bar. They are often used in conjunction with a spirit measure.

Store-and-pour containers

1 L and 2 L juice/milk containers are used for fast access to mixers. The shape and size make it easier to both store and pour. They are often fitted with coloured lids and caps for easy identification.

Glass dunker

A glass dunker is used to clean fruit juice or cream residue from glasses. It is generally used before washing glasses in the glasswasher.

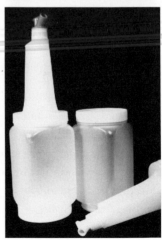

Salt rimmer

A multi-tiered salt and sugar rimmer is now common in many bars, providing speedy access when frosting glasses.

Straw caddy

A container that holds long and/or short straws, protecting them from unhygienic elements.

Rapid opener

A rapid opener is used to decork wine bottles rapidly, and is commonly found in bars with large-volume wine sales.

Glassware

Choosing the right glassware is a vital element when preparing a mixed drink or cocktail if it is to be invitingly presented and give satisfaction to the customer.

Glassware has a special affinity for liquid, enhancing its appearance and ensuring the full flavour appreciation.

There are certain conventions for choosing the right glass for the specific drink. A guide is provided below, with examples of the types of drinks usually served in each glass. (Some sizes are approximate, and may vary according to supplier.)

Shot glass

30 mL (1 fl oz)

Used for straight spirit shots and layered shots, e.g. B52.

Port/sherry glass

60 mL (2 fl oz)

Used for fortified wine, e.g. port, sherry.

Spirit/rocks/tumbler/old-fashioned glass

240 mL (8 fl oz)

Used for general spirits and mixed drinks as well as some cocktails, e.g. Black Russian.

Soda/highball/Collins glass

360 mL (12 fl oz)

Used for built non-alcoholic drinks (juice) as well as some cocktails, e.g. Harvey Wallbanger. The highball is also used for long or double spirits.

Wine/tulip glass

200 mL (7 fl oz)

Used for wine some wine-based cocktails, e.g. Kir.

Champagne/flute glass

150 mL (5 fl oz)

Used for champagne and champagne cocktails. Also used for small cocktails that are shaken and strained, e.g. Whisky Sour.

Brandy balloon/snifter

300 mL (10 fl oz)

Used for brandy and cognac. Also used for some cocktails and premium liqueurs 'on the rocks', e.g. Orgasm.

Special coffee

300 mL (10 fl oz)

Used for hot liqueur coffees, e.g. Irish coffee.

Colada glass

360 mL (12 fl oz)

Used for shaken and built cocktails, e.g. Pina Colada, mocktails.

(Coupette Margarita glass)

425 mL (14 fl oz)

Used for frozen cocktails and shaken drinks, e.g. Strawberry Margarita.

Hurricane

450 mL (15 fl oz)

Used for either blended cocktails or cocktails built over ice, e.g. Strawberry Daiquiri, Mai Tai.

Martini (small)

150 mL (5 fl oz)

Mainly used for cocktails that are stirred, e.g. Martini.

Martini (large)

300 mL (10 fl oz)

Used for drinks that are shaken and strained, e.g., Golden Dream, Shaken Margarita.

Pílsner

425 mL (14 fl oz)

Long glass used for beer.

Standard beer

300 mL (10 fl oz)

Beer glass sizes vary depending on the state or territory.

Dry goods

Items apart from alcoholic and non-alcoholic beverages and garnishes are referred to as 'dry goods'. These are important for good bar service and include:

Long and short straws	Used for stirring drinks as well as drinking. Straws also keep lipstick off the rims of the glasses.
Napkins and coasters	To absorb moisture, provide buffer for glassware, and customer use.
Toothpicks	Used for spearing garnishes and for customer use.
Glass cloths	To clean and polish glasses.
Cocktail/drinks list	Suggestively sells mixed drinks and cocktails to customers.

CHAPTER

Preparing for service

If you fail to prepare – prepare to fail!

The 'opening' bartender is responsible for the smooth running of the bar during the shift. If there are not enough garnishes cut or not enough stock on hand, the opening bartender may be held accountable.

A bar that is not opened correctly will have trouble maintaining continuity of service and this will frustrate staff members. The opening bartender has a responsibility to ensure that none of the 'basics' run out (for example, straws) and that customer service is not interrupted.

The 'closing' bartender is responsible for the cleanliness and order of the bar in preparation for the next shift. If a bar is closed badly the night before, the opening bartender may have to spend time finishing what should have been the previous night's duties. This may cause a delay in opening, and customers being turned away or asked to wait.

Procedures manual

Every bar should have a set of instructions detailing how to most effectively set up, maintain and run the bar. A procedures manual provides essential information on the bar's operational aspects that would otherwise take weeks, maybe months, to learn. By providing all information necessary to bring new staff members up to speed on key aspects of the bar's operations, valuable time is saved in the induction process.

The manual should be kept in the bar in a handy location for easy reference. Copies should be provided for staff upon commencement of employment and include:

▼ Opening and closing procedures,
▼ Bar par levels and back-up supplies checklist
▼ Bar maps and diagrams
▼ Product and price lists
▼ Cocktail lists
▼ General cleaning duties

The manual should be updated as new products come into the bar and cocktail lists change. Opening and closing procedures and cleaning rosters should be amended when new or better ways of completing the tasks are found.

The procedures manual might include a 'mission statement' for the venue. The mission statement summarises the overall objectives for the venue. The mission statement acts to bring everyone under the same banner – from managers to kitchen hands.

Example of a mission statement: 'To constantly exceed customer expectations through the provision of friendly, fast, professional service.'

Opening and closing duties

A straightforward set of opening and closing duties should be specified for all relevant bar staff to assist them in setting up and breaking down the bar in the fastest and most complete manner possible.

As a bartender gets more familiar with the bar, he or she may make adjustments to the procedures to improve the set-up or break-down time.

One method of prioritising the jobs at hand is to split the opening and closing jobs into two categories:

▼ Big jobs – jobs ideally completed when no customers are present
▼ Small jobs – jobs that can be completed while customers are present

Example of opening and closing duties

Opening duties

BIG JOBS   Turn on lights/coffee machine/glasswasher
Put floor mats down/prepare garbage bins and cleaning equipment
Put away all stock – check par levels* and replenish
Clean bar-top/put ashtrays out
Arrange chairs and tables

SMALL JOBS   Count float
Check juices/sodas
Arrange glassware
Prepare garnishes
Top up bar accompaniments
Fill ice well

*A par level is a set amount of backup stock kept in the bar

Closing duties

SMALL JOBS   Marry up (amalgamate) semi-full bottles
Bag up extra change
Clean and rack all glassware
Put fresh garnishes away
Empty ice well

BIG JOBS   Wipe down bar-top/tables
Stack chairs
Clean bar mats
Clean coffee machine and switch off
Clean glasswasher and switch off
Mop floor
Count takings

Bar par levels/back-up supplies

Par levels refer to the amount of backup stock kept in the bar or storeroom. The levels are set according to the demand for particular products (i.e. a fast-moving line such as house bourbon will have a higher par level compared with a slow-moving line such as Campari).

The par sheet in a bar should cover all products that are required on hand in the bar, including alcoholic products such as beer, wine and spirits; non-alcoholic products such as orange juice and cream; and dry goods such as straws and napkins.

Back-up supplies checklist

☑ Garnishes

Full tray of lemons and limes at service station plus backup lemons and limes stored in a fridge close at hand.

☑ Juices

Full juice containers stored at service station, backup orange juice, pineapple juice and other juices decanted into user-friendly containers and stored in a fridge close at hand.

☑ Spirits and liqueurs

Spirits full and wiped down – par level stock checked. Lids of bottles may be twisted to break the seals for convenient opening during the shift.

☑ Bottled beer

Bar fridges fully stocked. Backup beer and wine should be put on ice or into a fridge to provide cold reserves at a moment's notice.

☑ Wine

White house wine decorked and stored in fridge. Red house wine decorked and kept on a convenient shelf. House sparkling wine may have the foil removed and the ringlet exposed for ease of opening.

☑ Straws and napkins

Full straw and napkin caddies placed on the bar. Backup straws and napkins bundled up and stored in the bar for easy access.

☑ Tea towels

Bartenders should either carry tea towels or have them close at hand to keep their hands and the bar dry. Spare tea towels are stored in a cupboard close at hand.

☑ Money

Float drawer with sufficient coinage at start of the shift. Backup change checked off at the start of the shift and stored in a secure location. Ensure denominations are sorted in common bundles for easy identification.

☑ Draught beer

Popular beers coupled with backup kegs so as not to run out during a shift. Beers taps are checked and run off if necessary prior to the shift commencing.

General cleaning duties

A common saying in the hospitality industry is 'Time to lean – time to clean!' It is popular with venue owners or managers who want to keep their bar staff productive and on their toes. There are many reasons for maintaining a clean bar. Health issues are paramount. It is vital to ensure that all spills and drip trays are cleaned spotlessly.

A well-organised cleaning roster minimises the possibilities of infections, pest infestations and accidents. It is a good idea to spread the work out fairly among the staff. These jobs are usually performed on the off-peak shift.

The cleaning roster should cover each key area of the bar over one week. Jobs such as chemical washing of glassware are fairly big jobs that should be completed during the day, whereas on busy nights there should be little or no cleaning rostered. Cleaning jobs should be spread among several staff so that all cleaning is not left to one staff member.

Typical weekly bar cleaning duties

☑ Fridges

Often water collects at the bottom of the fridges as drainage lines get blocked. Fridge bottoms should be cleared of all water and left dry. Spills should be cleaned up immediately. Fridge doors and seals should also be cleaned weekly.

☑ Glasswashers

Glasswashers should be cleaned thoroughly. Points to check are: detergent level (Has it run out?), drainage hole (Is it blocked with debris?), inside corners (Is there any broken glass?).

☑ Free-pourers

It is important to keep free-pourers clean and running smoothly. They should be soaked weekly in hot water (nightly in some bars) with some fresh lemon juice in it. This dissolves built-up sugars, etc. When cleaning pourers, bottles should be capped or covered to keep insects out.

☑ Mirrors/glass

Display mirrors and glass behind the bar should be cleaned weekly. Make sure that no smudges or marks remain.

☑ Back bar bottles

Dusty or sticky bottles reflect badly on the business. Back bar bottles should be cleaned and polished weekly.

☑ Coffee machines

Coffee machines should be kept clean and polished. A special cleaning powder is available to flush out stale coffee in the lines. The steaming spout and drip tray should also be wiped down and kept clean.

☑ Glassware

Glasses are usually polished daily, and it is advisable to clean them thoroughly every week or so. A chemical cleanser should be used to remove tough stains (e.g. lipstick) and make them spotlessly clean.

☑ Beer lines

Since beer is a 'living' product, if it not kept clean it has a natural tendency to deteriorate. To avoid yeast building up in the lines, the beer lines are flushed weekly with water and then detergent. Beer drinkers are not impressed if beer looks and smells dirty.

☑ Drip trays and stainless areas

Although drip trays and stainless steel areas are generally cleaned daily, they should also be thoroughly cleaned weekly, with great attention to detail. When closing a bar for the day, it is easy to miss spots in the hurry to get out. This job is best done early in the week during the day.

Preparing garnishes

Cutting basic garnishes

Fruit is the most common garnish, with the lemon slice being the most popular. Some bars use limes regularly as a garnish, perhaps costing a little more, but adding more to the perceived value of the drink.

Below is a step-by-step guide to preparing the most common garnishes.

Use tongs when handling the fruit for hygiene reasons. A set of short-handled tongs should be kept on each side of the garnish tray so that the bartender can access the fruit with both hands.

Slice (lemon/lime/orange)

Equipment needed

> Cutting board
> Fruit knife
> Garnish tray

▼ Wash fruit and remove any stickers.
▼ Lay on side and cut off both ends, leaving as much flesh on fruit as possible.
▼ Cut in half (or into quarters if fruit is large) lengthwise and lay pieces flesh-down on board.
▼ Slice even, parallel cuts along fruit 3–5 mm apart.

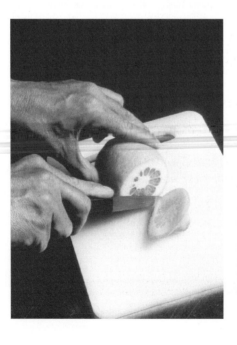
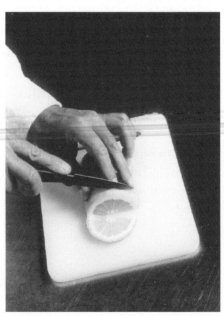

Wedge (lemon/lime)

Equipment needed

Cutting board
Fruit knife

▼ Wash fruit and remove any stickers.
▼ Lay on side and cut in half lengthwise.
▼ Lay halves peel-down on the board.
▼ Cut each half into 3–4 wedges.

4 3

Twist (lemon/lime/orange)

Equipment needed

Cutting board
Fruit channeller

▼ Wash fruit and remove any stickers.
▼ Hold in hand and press channeller on fruit skin firmly.
▼ Turn fruit with hand.
▼ Prepare twists approximately 5 cm long.

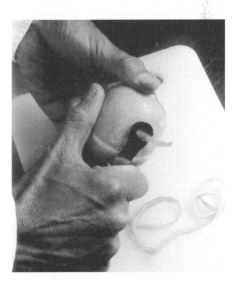

Twists my be tied into a knot for garnishing purposes if desired.

Wheel (lemon/lime/orange)

Equipment needed

    Cutting board
    Fruit knife

▼ Wash fruit and remove any stickers.
▼ Cut off one end, leaving as much flesh on fruit as possible.
▼ Slice a full circle from fruit.
▼ Make small incision to mount on glass.

Frosted glass (salt/sugar/coconut)

Equipment needed

    Salt/sugar rimmer
    Glass

▼ Wet rim of glass with fruit or sponge soaked in cordial.
▼ Place glass downwards on saucer/salt rimmer and rotate until rim is covered.
▼ Remove glass and flick off any excess.

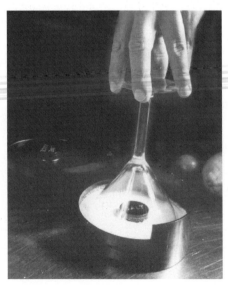

Single/double cherry
Equipment needed

Fruit knife
Cutting board

▼ Lay cherry on side and cut small slit on the bottom.
▼ Mount on glass

Strawberry kiss
Equipment needed

Fruit knife
Cutting board

▼ Lay strawberry on side and cut off top (stem).
▼ Cut in half lengthwise.
▼ Press backs of two halves onto rim of glass, side by side.

Strawberry fan
Equipment needed

Fruit knife
Cutting board

▼ Lay strawberry on side and cut three or four slits in fruit running from just under stem to base.
▼ Fan strawberry out with fingers and place on top of blended mixture, or cut a slit and mount on side of glass.

Pineapple segment
Equipment needed

    Fruit knife
    Cutting board

▼ Wash fruit.
▼ Cut off base of pineapple.
▼ Cut a slice about 1–2 cm thick.
▼ Lay pineapple circle flat and cut into eight segments.
▼ Make small incision in bottom corner of each segment for mounting on glass.

Pineapple flag
Equipment needed

    Fruit knife
    Cutting board
    Toothpick

▼ Prepare pineapple segment and mount on glass (see above).
▼ Attach a cherry to two pineapple leaves using a toothpick.
▼ Press cherry and leaves into pineapple segment.

UFO

Equipment needed

Fruit knife
Cutting board
Toothpicks

▼ Prepare orange wheel (as explained on page 44).
▼ Using two toothpicks, attach cherry to centre of orange wheel.
▼ Mount garnish on side of glass by pressing rim of glass between the two toothpicks.

Once the garnishes have been cut, they should be stored in a garnish tray. They should be kept grouped tightly together to prevent oxidisation. Garnishes stored correctly last up to twice as long as those thrown loosely into the garnish tray.

Straws can be considered a garnish, as they complement drinks and act as stirrers, helping to mix the various flavours together.

Mixed drinks garnishing guide

Choosing the correct garnish for a mixed drink is an important part of the finished drink. Serving drinks with wrong or missing garnishes detracts from the quality of service. The following is a guide.

White spirits generally have a lemon slice, except when mixed with:

Orange juice	Orange garnish
Tonic	Lime garnish
Cranberry juice	Lime garnish
Pineapple juice	No garnish

Note: White spirits have a lemon garnish even when mixed with cola.

Brown spirits generally have no garnish.

Garnishing guidelines

Key
L = Lemon   Li = Lime   O = Orange   S = Slice
W = Wedge   C = Circle   X = Don't mix well!

	Cola	Lemonade	Tonic	Squash	Ginger ale	Diet Cola	Lime and soda	Orange juice	Pineapple juice	Cranberry juice	Lemon juice	Grapefruit juice	Watermelon juice
Bourbon	No garnish												
Scotch	No garnish												
Vodka		LS	LiW	LS	LiW	LS	LS	OS		LiW	LS	LiW	LiW
Gin		LS	LiW	LS	LiW		LS	OS		LiW	LS	LiW	LiW
Rum (dark)	No garnish												
Rum (white)	LS	LS	LiW	LS	LiW	LS	LS	OS		LiW	LS	LiW	LiW
Brandy		LS		LS			LS						
Tequila		LS	LiW	LS	LiW	LS	LS	OS		LiW	LS	LiW	LiW
Midori	LS	LS	LiW	LS	LS	LS	LS	OS		LiW	LS	LiW	LS
Campari		OS	LiW		LiW		OS	OS		LiW	LS	LiW	LiW
Ouzo	No garnish												
Vermouth		LS	LS	LS	LS	LS	LS	OS		LS	LS	LS	LS
Cointreau		OS	OS	LS	LS	LS	OS	OS		OS	LS	LiW	LiW

Specific fruit garnishes may vary from venue to venue.

Product knowledge

Good salespeople are passionate about their products.

Spirits

Spirits are produced by the process of distillation, which separates the ethyl alcohol from the other substances by heating. The clear spirit is then sometimes flavoured, coloured or aged in wood. Most bars offer a range of spirits, from cheap 'house' spirits to more expensive 'top-shelf' spirits. Bartenders should be familiar with the full range of each spirit category, enabling them to recommend higher quality alternatives if appropriate.

Spirit pricing categories

Bottom shelf   (referred to as house, rack or basic spirits) – least expensive and lesser quality.

Mid shelf   (referred to as call spirits) – slightly more expensive, well-known brands.

Top shelf   (referred to as premium, deluxe or exotic spirits) – most expensive and highest quality.

For example, Scotch whisky is represented by at least one brand per 'shelf':

Bottom shelf   Bells 8 Year Old

Mid shelf   Johnnie Walker Red Label

Top shelf   Johnnie Walker Black Label

Although spirit categories may be divided into 'shelves', this does not indicate their appropriate positioning in the bar. See Chapter 11, Product and Equipment Placement.

Spirit summary chart

Name	Country of origin	Approximate % alcohol by volume*	Flavour/ description	Shelf brand examples B = Bottom M = Middle T = Top
Bourbon	USA	37.5–50.5	Rich, sweetish, caramel overtones	B – Real McCoy M – Jim Beam T – Wild Turkey
Scotch whisky	Scotland	40–43	Pungent, dry, smokey	B – Bells 8 Year Old M – Johnnie Walker Red T – Johnnie Walker Black
Vodka	Russia/ Poland	37.5–40	Odourless, weak, flavourless	B – Cossack M – Stolichnaya T – Smirnoff Black
Gin	England Netherlands	37.5–40	Juniper and citrus infused bouquet	B – Vickers M – Gordons T – Tanqueray
Rum (white)	West Indies	37.5–57.5	Light, dry, slightly sweet	B – Benleigh M – Bacardi

Spirit summary chart (continued)

Name	Country of origin	Approximate % alcohol by volume*	Flavour/ description	Shelf brand examples B = Bottom M = Middle T = Top
Rum (dark)	West Indies	37.5–57.5	Rich, sweet, caramelised	B – Bundaberg UP T – Bundaberg OP
Brandy	France	37.5–40	Sweet bouquet, complex	B – Tolleys T – Hennessy
Tequila (white)	Mexico	37.5–40	Subtle, muted bouquet	B – El Toro M – Cuervo Gold T – Cuervo 1800
Tequila (mezcal)	Mexico	37.5–50	Bitter, raw, strong	T – Dos Eckes
Irish whiskey	Ireland	37.5–40	Smooth, mellow, light	M – Jameson T – Bush Mills
Canadian whisky	Canada	37.5–40	Smooth, sweetish	M – Canadian Club/Seagrams VO
Tennessee whiskey	USA	37.5–43	Complex, full bodied, mellow	M – Jack Daniel's T – George Dickel
Ouzo	Greece	37.5–40	Pungent aniseed flavour and aroma	M – Olympic

* In Australia spirits are measured by alcohol by volume (ABV), indicating the percentage of alcohol in the container. The term 'overproof' refers to spirits that are more than 57.1% alcohol hy volume, and 'under-proof' less than this percentage.

Liqueurs

A liqueur is a spirit made with other ingredients added to it – such as sugar, flavours and colours. There are two types of liqueurs found in the modern bar: proprietary and generic.

Proprietary liqueurs (e.g. Cointreau) are 'top-shelf' liqueurs that are available around the world. They are produced using high-quality production methods and ingredients. Generic liqueurs (e.g. triple sec) are seen as cheaper substitutes for the proprietary liqueurs and some are produced locally.

The modern bar stocks both kinds of liqueurs, providing a range of options for the bartender to use when preparing mixed drinks and cocktails.

Liqueurs are generally used in combination with spirits but over the last few decades there has been significant growth in the drinking of liqueurs with straight mixers, e.g. Malibu and milk, Midori and lemonade.

Efficiency tip

Some bars stock only those liqueurs that sell on a fairly regular basis. It may not be worthwhile keeping a bottle in stock if it only sells one shot every month or two. Liqueurs can be expensive, and take up valuable shelf space that could be used for displaying other, faster-moving products.

Proprietary liqueurs

These are mostly imported more expensive liqueurs with a distinctive recipe, bottle shape and brand name.

Proprietary liqueurs summary chart

Name	Country of origin	% alcohol by volume	Flavour/description
Baileys	Ireland	17	Irish whiskey base, vanilla and cream
Cointreau	France	40	Sweet orange with herbs
Benedictine	France	43	Brandy base, citrus and herbs
Drambuie	Scotland	40	Scotch base, heather honey and herbs
Frangelico	Italy	24	Light hazelnut
Galliano	Italy	35	Vanilla with caramel, slight aniseed
Grand Marnier	France	40	Cognac base, sweet orange and herbs
Kahlua	Mexico	27	Rich coffee
Malibu	West Indies	21	Soft coconut
Midori	Japan	21	Sweet, honeydew melon
Pernod	France	40	Strong aniseed
Pimm's No. 1	England	40	Gin base, mixed berries
Southern Comfort	USA	38	Bourbon base, peaches
Tia Maria	West Indies	32	Rum base, light coffee
Mandarine Napoleon	France	25	Brandy base, mandarin flavour

Generic liqueurs

Generic liqueurs are cheaper liqueurs without a protected name, recipe or bottle shape. They are produced cheaply and priced competitively. Brands of generic liqueurs include Vok, Baitz and Seagram.

Having two liqueur categories in the bar enables substitution of cheaper generic liqueurs for more expensive proprietary liqueurs, lowering the cost of drink production.

For example, when making a Margarita the more expensive ingredient Cointreau can be substituted with its generic substitute, triple sec. Both have a similar orange flavour but the latter is less than half the price.

Generic liqueurs summary chart

Name	Approx % alcohol by volume	Flavour
Crème de cacao (white)	23	Chocolate
Crème de cacao (brown)	23	Chocolate
Crème de menthe (green)	23	Peppermint
Crème de menthe (white)	23	Peppermint
Crème de mure (white)	23	Blackberry
Crème de menthe (white)	23	Peppermint
Apricot brandy	23	Apricot
White curaçao	23	Orange
Blue curaçao	23	Orange
Orange curaçao	23	Orange
Triple sec	23	Orange
Cherry brandy	23	Cherry
Banana liqueur	23	Banana
Frais be bois	23	Strawberry
Mango liqueur	25	Mango
Crème de cassis	25	Blackcurrant
Peach schnapps	25	Peach
Butterscotch schnapps	25	Butterscotch
Sambuca	40	Licorice
Amaretto	27	Almond
Sloe gin	27	Sloe Berry

Substitution chart

Proprietary	Generic
Cointreau	Triple sec
Midori	Melon liqueur
Malibu	Coconut liqueur
Kahlua	Creme de café
Lena	Banana liqueur
Tia Maria	Crème de cacao

Spirit and liqueur compatibility

This section provides guidelines for combining spirits and liqueurs for the purposes of mixing cocktails.

White spirits

White spirits are the most versatile type of spirit for cocktail mixing purposes. The advantage of using spirits such as vodka and white rum as mixers is that they provide a fairly neutral alcohol base on which to build other flavours. Spirits such as gin and tequila are more strongly flavoured, and may sometimes predominate in a mixed drink.

Dark spirits

Dark spirits are by nature stronger in flavour than white spirits. Spirits such as bourbon and Scotch are harder to disguise with other liqueurs and mixers. Dark rum may be mixed with juices and fruit liqueurs because of its sweeter flavour.

Dark spirits such as brandy and rye whisky are medium-bodied and lighter in flavour than the others and are also more commonly used in cocktails.

Liqueurs

Liqueurs mix well with a variety of ingredients, and those with similar characteristics are most likely to be compatible. For example, fruit liqueurs mix well together, as do chocolate and coffee liqueurs. Although bartenders often break this rule to create new and different flavours, a safe rule of thumb is stay within the flavour category.

Common liqueur combinations

Baileys	Coffee chocolate/coffee liqueurs (e.g. Kahlua, crème de cacao, Frangelico)
Cointreau/triple sec	Most other liqueurs (e.g. Midori, Tia Maria, banana liqueur)
Crème de cacao	Chocolate/coffee liqueurs (e.g. Kahlua, Frangelico)
Crème de cassis	Fruit liqueurs (e.g. Midori, banana liqueur)
Crème de menthe	Heavily flavoured liqueurs (e.g. Baileys, Kahlua)
Curaçao	Most other liqueurs
Drambuie	Heavily flavoured liqueurs (e.g. Galliano, Kahlua)
Frangelico	Chocolate/coffee and cream liqueurs (e.g. Tia Maria, crème de cacao, Baileys) as well as some fruit liqueurs (e.g. banana liqueur)
Galliano	Fruit and/or chocolate liqueurs (e.g. Cointreau and crème de cacao)
Kahlua	Chocolate/coffee and cream liqueurs (e.g. crème de cacao, Baileys)
Malibu	Fruit and/or chocolate liqueurs (e.g. Midori, Tia Maria)
Midori	Fruit and/or coconut liqueurs (e.g. Malibu, banana liqueur)
Tia Maria	Chocolate/coffee liqueurs, some fruit (e.g. Baileys, crème de cacao, strawberry liqueur)

Bottled beer and ready-to-drink products

The term 'ready to drink' (RTD) refers to drinks that are prepackaged, chilled and ready for immediate consumption.

Bottled beer and ready-to-drink (RTD) products are becoming increasingly popular in Australian bars. Bottled beers have enjoyed rapid growth, as have pre-mixed drinks such as Stolichnaya Lemon Ruski and Smirnoff Baltik.

Bottled beverages are generally more profitable to serve than draught beer, as it is faster to serve and saves on wastage. It takes about three times longer to serve a glass of draft beer than to serve a beer in a bottle.

Bars need to be stocked to take advantage of market trends, and serving bottled beers and RTDs appeals to certain customers. Not doing so might lead to a decline in patronage as nearby competitors adapt to changes and reap the rewards.

Bottled beer

The demand for bottle beer has been steadily increasing in Australia. Customers often prefer bottled beer because it is more convenient to hold than a glass of draught beer, particularly in a crowded bar or nightclub environment. Some bars offer bottled beer with a glass, while others serve the bottle only.

Bottled beers may be classified as follows:

Light beer   Beer that contains less than 3 per cent alcohol by volume.

Local beer   Full-strength beer made in Australia (approximately 4.9% alcohol by volume).

Boutique beer   Full-strength beer made in smaller quantities with an emphasis on quality.

Imported beer   Full-strength beer imported from overseas, incurring excise tax and therefore costing more than beers produced locally.

Bottled beer and RTD summary chart

Category	Brand	Place of origin	Beverage description
Light beer	Foster's Light Ice	Vic	Lager
	Toohey's Blue Ice	NSW	Lager
	Cooper's Light	SA	Lager
	Foster's Special Lager	Vic	Lager
Local beer	Victoria Bitter	Vic	Lager
	XXXX Gold	Qld	Lager
	Swan	WA	Lager
	Toohey's Old	NSW	Stout
	Toohey's Dry	NSW	Lager
	Resch's	NSW	Lager
Boutique beer	Cascade	Tas	Pale ale
	Pikes	Tas	Lager
	James Boag's	Tas	Lager
	Redback	WA	Wheat beer
	Crown	Vic	Lager
	Cooper's Ale	SA	Ale
	Foster's Special	Vic	Lager
	Hahn Premium	NSW	Lager
Imported beer	Corona	Mexico	Lager
	Sol	Mexico	Lager
	Miller	USA	Lager
	Budweiser	USA	Lager
	Beck's	Germany	Lager
	Heineken	Holland	Lager
	Stella Artois	Belgium	Lager
	Peroni	Italy	Lager
	Steinlager	NZ	Lager
	Guinness	Ireland	Stout
Pre-mix	Bacardi Breezer	UK	Watermelon, citrus, orange
	Bundaberg and cola	Australia	Dark rum and cola
	Johnnie Walker Red Label and cola	Australia/ Scotland	Scotch and cola
	Stolichnaya Lemon Ruski	Australia	Vodka and squash
	Smirnoff Baltik	Australia	Vodka and grapefruit/citrus
Alcoholic soda	Sub Zero	Australia	Original, Lime, Pink Grapefruit
Cider/wine cooler	West Coast Cooler	Australia	Carbonated wine and flavourings
	Strongbow	Australia	Fermented apples

Pre-mixed drinks

Some bars stock bottles or cans of pre-mixed drinks as a way of speeding up service (e.g. UDL, Bundaberg and Cola). Although pre-mix has a higher unit cost to the retailer, improved bar productivity may make its use viable.

Alcoholic sodas

Alcoholic sodas are a fairly new category in the liquor market, probably best known through the market leader Sub Zero. The alcoholic base for these drinks is usually fermented molasses (sugar), which is combined with flavouring and carbonated.

Ciders and wine coolers

Ciders and wine coolers have been the long-time beer substitute for people who don't drink spirits or don't like the taste of beer, or find the sweet, fruity taste of ciders and wine coolers a lot more appealing.

This category has been somewhat outstripped by the new, fancy alcoholic sodas category, but it still manages to maintain a significant share of the market. Strongbow cider and West Coast cooler are two of the more popular brands.

Wine and wine-based products

Per capita sales of wine-based products have been growing steadily, while some other major liquor categories have either remained fairly static or are in decline.

Bottled wine is becoming more popular in bars, with many bars offering a selection of wines by the glass, allowing customers to sample different wines with a small outlay.

Still wine

Wine is produced by fermenting grapes to convert fruit sugar in into alcohol using yeast.

Still wine is wine that does not contain carbon dioxide. It is the most popular form of wine in Australia and is predominantly sold in bottles and casks.

There are two methods of labelling still wine in Australia: *varietal* (meaning the wine is named after the grape) and *generic* (meaning the wine is named after a style or region).

Varietal examples

White Chardonnay, Sauvignon Blanc, Semillon

Red Cabernet Sauvignon, Shiraz, Pinot Noir

59

When a blend of two or more varieties of grapes is used in a wine, they are listed on the label in the order of the quantities contained in the bottle. For example, a Semillon Sauvignon Blanc is made from a mixture of Semillon grapes with a lesser amount of Sauvignon Blanc grapes.

Generic examples

White Chablis, white burgundy, moselle

Red Claret, burgundy, rosé

Sparkling wine and champagne

What used to be known as champagne in Australia is now known commercially as 'sparkling wine'. The word champagne can now only be used on labels of wine that is produced in the Champagne region of France.

Sparkling wine is produced by dissolving carbon dioxide into the wine, in a process similar to the production of soft drinks.

Champagne has the carbon dioxide introduced naturally as part of the fermentation process, the most common method being méthode champenoise, whereby the gas forms in the bottle.

Méthode champenoise was invented in the late seventeenth century by Dom Perignon, still a well-known brand of champagne today.

Sparkling wines and champagnes are commonly labelled in the terms of their 'dryness':

Brut   The driest style of sparkling wine or champagne

Extra sec A very dry style

Sec   A dry style

Demi sec   A medium-dry style

Doux   A sweet style

Fortified wine

Fortified wines have a spirit base added, increasing the alcohol content and changing the flavour. Fortified wines can be grouped into two categories, according to normal time for serving.

Aperitif wine

An aperitif is a drink served before meals to stimulate the appetite by engaging the gastric juices and preparing the taste buds for food. Appetisers are usually served in short glasses and contain between of 15 and 22 per cent alcohol by volume. Examples include vermouth, Dubonnet and sherry.

Dessert wine

Dessert wines are sweet, full-bodied wines that are mainly served at the conclusion of a meal or with dessert. They may be sweet white wines, or fortified wines. Port is still the most popular fortified dessert wine in Australia, traditionally served in a 60 mL port glass. The word 'port' comes form the town of Oporto in Portugal, where it was originally produced. The main types of port are:

Ruby   A basic 'table' port. This port is a light ruby colour and is not aged.

Tawny   A wood-matured style. Often a blend of different vintages.

Vintage A quality port from a dated single batch.

Draught beer

Draught beer continues to be the drink of choice for many Australians. Over the years there have been significant advances in draught beer technology, with suppliers endeavoring to remedy problems such as wastage and space management. Modern draught beer systems are user-friendly, space efficient and aesthetically pleasing.

Beer production

Beer is brewed using the following components:

Barley   A grain
Sugar   Added if insufficient sugar in the grain
Hops   Flavouring agent
Yeast   Catalyst for conversion

There are two types of yeast used in the brewing of beer: Top-fermented yeast, which produces a darker style of beer (e.g. ale) Bottom-fermented yeast, which produces a lighter type of beer (e.g. lager).

The qualities of a good beer

There are certain qualities that a consumer looks for in a beer (often without realising it). A beer that is not chilled enough or is flat (lacks bubbles) might be brought back to the bar to be exchanged. The following elements determine the quality of a beer.

Temperature

Beer in Australia has is best served between 2 and 3 degrees Celsius, and even colder in hot weather.

Clarity

Unless it is an ale or stout, beer should be translucent or see-through. If a draught beer is cloudy or has unwanted sediment, there may be something wrong with the beer lines.

Sparkle

A lack of bubbles is the biggest indicator that something is wrong with either the glass or the beer lines. The bubbles should rise from the bottom of the glass – bubbles clustered on the side of a glass are generally an indication of a dirty glass.

Head

In Australia beer is served with a head of approximately 1–2 centimetres. The head should stay on the beer, depending on serving conditions, for 5 minutes before dissipating. A head that disappears very quickly indicates a bad pour or lack of carbonation.

Lacing

Lacing refers to the marks that are left by the head on the glass as the beer is consumed. An empty glass that has lacing all the way down indicates that the beer is fresh and that the glassware is clean.

Flavour

Beer should be refreshing to the palate. A bad taste or odour is usually a sign that the beer lines need to be cleaned.

Types of draught beer

Lager/new

Most Australian beers are lagers, or bottom-fermented beers. The term 'new' is sometimes used to describe lighter style of beer. Lagers come in dry, low-alcohol and premium styles.

Ale/old

Australian ales are sometimes referred to as 'old'. Ale is a top-fermented beer with a small amount of roasted barley added to the brew.

Stout

Stout is an ale that has extra roasted barley added.

Beer 'cocktails'

Beer cocktails are simple mixes of beer with other ingredients. The most common in many bars is the shandy.

Shandy	Lager and lemonade (with lemonade poured first)
50/50	Half ale or 'old' beer and half lager or 'new' beer
Black and Tan	Half stout (dark ale) and half lager
Black Velvet	Half stout and half champagne or sparking wine
Depth Charge	30 mL Drambuie dropped into a glass of beer
Lager and Lime	Lager with lime cordial
Lager and Black	Lager with blackcurrant cordial

Non-alcoholic supplies

Traditional bars tend to stock only non-alcoholic supplies required by their customers, e.g. orange juice or milk. As tastes change, bars are experimenting with new non-alcoholic mixers in order to capture their customers' imagination.

One of the new mixers making a 'splash' is cranberry juice, a highly popular cocktail mixer in the USA and now gaining popularity in bars around Australia.

Fruit and juices

A good supply of fresh fruit and juices is important for the mixing of quality cocktails. The following juices and fruit should be standard in today's cocktail bar.

Fruit	Juices
Oranges	Orange juice
Lemons	Lemon juice
Limes	Pineapple juice
Bananas	Tomato juice
Strawberries	Cranberry juice
Pineapple	Grapefruit juice
Passionfruit	Guava juice
Mangos	Mango juice
Peaches	Apple juice
Raspberries	
Kiwifruit	

These are just some of the fruits and juices that can be stocked in a bar. There is no limit to types of fruits and juices that can be mixed in cocktails The availability of fresh fruit changes according to the season – so why not make the most of it while it is at its best.

Sodas and other mixers

Most bars are equipped with post-mix (soda) guns or units, which provide a ready supply of soda mixers. Other essential ingredients such as milk and cream are not as readily available in bars but should be kept close at hand. Standard sodas and other mixers found in most Australian bars are:

Sodas	Post-mix code
Cola	C
Lemonade	L
Ginger ale	G
Tonic	T
Squash	Q
Soda	S

Other mixers
Milk
Cream
Coconut cream
Ginger beer

Energy drinks

Energy drinks such as Red Bull have seen dramatic growth in recent years. They are commonly sold as an alcohol substitute but can also be mixed with spirits (e.g. Vodka Bull) as well as included in some cocktails.

Cordials and syrups

A wide variety of cordials and syrups gives bartenders easy access to liquids with high sugar content for sweetening mixed drinks or taking the edge off an alcohol 'bite'.

With the growing availability of flavoured syrups such as those available in the Monin range, expensive liqueurs can be replaced with cheaper non-alcoholic substitutes. This makes it possible to mix half-strength cocktails and offer them to customers at a reduced price.

The following cordials and syrups are recommended as standard ingredients:

Cordials

Lemon cordial

Lime cordial

Raspberry cordial

Grenadine

Lime cordial and Sugar (Gomme) Syrup generally serve the same purpose, as they are both sweeteners (lime cordial is popular in soda drinks). Raspberry cordial and grenadine syrup are interchangeable.

Syrups and mixers

Sugar (Gomme) Syrup
2 cups sugar
1 cup hot water

Bring to boil in saucepan or mix in blender then allow to cool and decant into user-friendly bottle or container.

Sour Mix
1 cup Sugar Syrup
1 cup fresh lemon/lime juice
3 egg whites

Add all ingredients to user-friendly container and shake to mix.

Half and Half
2 cups milk
2 cups running cream

Add all ingredients to user-friendly container and shake to mix.

Strawberry/Mango Purée
Fresh or frozen strawberries/mangoes
1 cup Sugar Syrup

Mix all ingredients in blender and decant into user-friendly container.

Consumable supplies

Condiments (consumable supplies) differentiate a well-equipped bar from the rest. A checklist for the modern cocktail bar would include:

Olives	Angostura Bitters	Coffee beans
Celery salt	Cinnamon	Eggs
Cube sugar	Cucumber	Grated chocolate
Honey	Maraschino cherries	Mint
Nutmeg	Salt and pepper	Tabasco sauce
Worcestershire sauce	Caster sugar	

CHAPTER **8**

Customer service

Effective selling increases revenue as well as improving customer service.

A bartender is a salesperson and, as with all sales positions, good communications skills are required to sell effectively. Some customers know what they want before they arrive at the bar and are ready to order. Others arrive at a bar and make up their mind right then and there. In either case, the bartender can influence exactly what the customer chooses to purchase, often being regarded as an expert.

Not only can a bartender guide the customer's drinking preferences, but by being friendly and helpful, he or she can promote customer satisfaction.

Customer service

Good service generates return customers, but sloppy or unfriendly service is likely to drive customers away.

It is important for bartenders to realise that their jobs are being maintained by customer loyalty. In short, the customer pays their wages. If adequate service is not provided by a staff member, customers have a right to feel hard-done-by, because they have not received the service they paid for.

Customer needs

When customers come to a bar, they expect courtesy, prompt service, nice tasting drinks and value for money. If one or more of these elements is missing, they may be disappointed because their expectations have not been met.

In order to provide good customer service, a bartender needs to understand basic customer needs and expectations

Good customer service means meeting or exceeding all of the above needs. This is the key to generating return customers, and earning tips!

Customer needs	Bartender qualities
Courtesy	Be polite
Understanding	Take the time to listen
Sensitivity	Show empathy – be aware
Tact	Judge the situation
Relaxation	Do not crowd/rush
Value	Do not oversell
Service	Make customers feel good
EXCEEDING EXPECTATIONS	
Entertainment	Be interesting
Humour	Make it fun
Thoughtfulness	Pre-empting needs, e.g. tissues for sneezes
Care	Listening and consoling

Customer communication

A good way to stay in control of the bar when busy is to constantly search for eye contact (usually indicating that the customer wants the bartender's attention). A good bartender uses peripheral vision when working – constantly looking up and down the bar.

Once eye contact is established, there are several forms of communication that the bartender may employ, ranging from a nod of the head to a hand signal indicating to the customer that service won't be long.

It may be appropriate for a bartender to keep talking to customers while they are waiting to be served. By using communication skills it is possible to keep customers happy, even when they may have to wait a while for service.

In a busy bar, acknowledging customers immediately helps the bartender to keep track of who needs service and makes the customers feel more comfortable while waiting.

The bartender may even inform the customer of the situation by saying something like: 'I've just got an order for a couple of cocktails but I shouldn't be too long.' This will keep the customer satisfied for a few minutes as they know they will be served shortly. On the other hand, bartenders who do not communicate effectively may end up facing a bar full of anxiously waiting customers.

Relationship building

The key to satisfying most customers' needs is to build a rapport with them. While being friendly is fine, it comes a lot more naturally when respect exists between the bartender and the customers. A good bartender knows the regular customers and treats them as friends.

Relationship building helps to provide repeat business, with regular customers becoming an important source of revenue.

Building relationships with customers

Acknowledge the customer by name.
'Hi Bill, how's things?'

Have the customer's drink committed to memory.
'The usual?'

Ask open questions and listen.
'How's work been ...'

Use small talk.
'It's been quite busy tonight.'

Introduce good customers to other members of staff.
'Have you met Cindy, she usually works on Saturdays?'

Open questions

By asking 'open' questions (questions that begin with who, what, where, etc.), a bartender can involve the customer in a conversation. This sort of communication also helps customers to relax.

Open questions start with ...

Who?
Why?
What?
Where?

These types of question are likely to involve the customer in a conversation.

Closed questions

Closed questions invite a yes/no answer and are not conducive to conversation, but can be used to close a sale. For example, 'Would you like a drink?' or 'Are you being served?'.

A bartender should always try to speak to customers on a level that they understand. Avoid being too smart or confronting.

Order taking

Good order-taking techniques improve customer service. Being able to smile, greet and take an order from a customer in a fast, efficient manner generally leads to increased customer satisfaction and a more profitable bar.

The initial contact (or first impression) tells a customer a lot about the bartender and the venue. If the bartender is rude or inattentive, the customer may well assume that the whole venue is the same. On the other hand, if the bartender is forthcoming and friendly the customer is likely to feel good about being there and will have a positive view of the venue.

Taking an order – step by step

▼ Acknowledge customers as soon as possible on arrival to the bar.
   'I'll be with you shortly.'

▼ Greet customers in a polite and friendly manner.
   'Hi. How are you this evening?'

▼ Wait for a response then ask a question for the purpose of taking an order.
  'What would you like to drink?' (Open question)

▼ If there is a slight hesitation, it may be appropriate to suggestively sell to the customer.
  e.g. *'We've got a special on Smirnoff tonight. It's only $3'.*

▼ If there is no hesitation and a drink order is taken, help guide the drinking experience by adding value to the drink order.
  'Would you like fresh lime in that?', *'Would you like a straw?'*, *'Tall glass?'* ...

▼ Make the order.

Efficiency tips

Orders should be combined to increase efficiency. It is all too common for bartenders to take single drink orders from customers waiting at a busy bar – not bothering to check what the next person in line may want.

By combining orders, a bartender can effectively keep control of a portion of the bar at a time – rather than just individuals.

> When starting to combine orders, begin by remembering 2–3 drinks and then increase the number over time.
> See Chapter 12, Multiple Drink Mixing for more information on preparing combined orders.

Suggestive selling

Suggestive selling can be used if the bartender feels that it necessary to 'lead' the customer – giving a helping hand to decide.

Selling techniques are used more frequently when a bar is building up to, or just moving away from, a peak service period. By selling higher priced items in slower periods a bar can improve its average revenue.

> During the peak service period it is usually more profitable to sell the cheaper or 'house' spirits. The rule of thumb is: sell from the front bar when busy and the back bar when quiet.

A typical bar shift builds slowly to the peak service period (which may last for a few hours), then drops off.

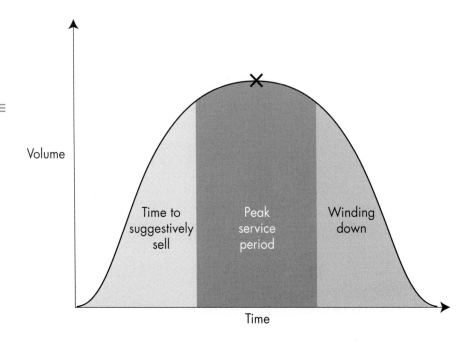

Suggestive selling is a 'soft sell', with the customer never feeling pressured throughout the service.

The two most common types of selling used in a bar are the comparative sell and the up-sell.

The comparative sell

Comparative selling is a form of suggestive selling used once a customer has given an order. It is especially useful when a product is out of stock and a replacement is suggested in order to ensure the sale. If the bartender does not suggest a replacement, the customer's basic level of expectation may not be met.

The comparative sell – examples

A customer orders a drink that the bar either does not stock or has run out of.

Order	Heineken
Situation	Out of stock
Response	'Would you like a Peroni instead?'

Both Heineken and Peroni are full-flavoured imported beers)

A customer can't remember the name of a particular mixed drink and needs to describe it.

Order   Cocktail
Situation Can't remember name and describes drink
Response   'How about a Mudslide? It's very similar.'

The up-sell

Up-selling involves the bartender suggesting a substitute drink or product that is of a higher value than the customer's original order.

Bars benefit from up-selling in two ways. Firstly it provides a higher level of attentiveness and therefore better service through the customer's eyes. Secondly, it increases the average price of drinks sold, resulting in increased profit.

If each bartender in a busy bar 'up-sold' 10–20 drink orders a night, revenue would be increased by hundreds of dollars. There might also be an increase in indirect revenue from the resulting return business.

The up-sell – examples

A customer orders a drink out of habit.

Order   Gin and tonic
Situation Regular drink order
Response   'Is Gordons okay?

A customer wants a beer but is not sure which brand to choose.

Order   Bottle of champagne
Situation Special occasion
Response   'I've got some nice French champagne in the cooler.'

Often a customer will order from the first options presented. Start with top of the range and work down.

A word on tips ...

Tipping a waiter or bartender in Australia was once seen as unnecessary, but as the service industry has developed and matured, tipping has become an increasingly common practice in restaurants and bars. Tips are generally often given if a bartender has exceeded, or at the very least, met, all of the customer's expectations.

It is common for tips to be shared by all bartenders working the shift. Bartenders working less hours should get proportionately less tips. Glassies or bar-backs sometimes get a percentage of total bar tips (usually between 10 and 15 per cent).

Tips about tips

▼ Tips should never be put in a pocket. They should be kept in a container away from the register.

▼ Use a change plate when delivering customer change. This gives customers time to reflect on the service.

▼ Break change into smaller denominations (say $1 or 50 cents), as the customer may feel more inclined to tip if it is a smaller amount.

▼ Acknowledge the tip and thank the customer, letting them know it is appreciated. (This also indicates to other customers that tipping the bartender is welcome).

Preparing drinks

*Mixology is an artform practised by many —
perfected by few.*

Efficient bar practices

The efficient preparation of drinks is an essential step towards optimising bar productivity. Accuracy, timeliness and a good memory are part of a professional bartender's repertoire, leading to speedy service and satisfied customers.

Bartender efficiency requires intuition, coordination, practice and persistence. The following are some of the factors that affect a bartender's service speed.

Centralising the work

In a busy bar the bartender should ideally be centred at a workstation, with all equipment close at hand.

The bartender needs to stay at service station as much as possible, preparing drinks and talking to customers. Obviously, the bartender has to move out of the area to take orders, wipe the bar, etc. but he or she should return to the service station area as often as possible.

A bartender should try to face the customers to keep an eye on who is waiting for service. If the service station is left unattended, the bartender may not be able to see new customers arriving at the bar and this will affect customer service.

74

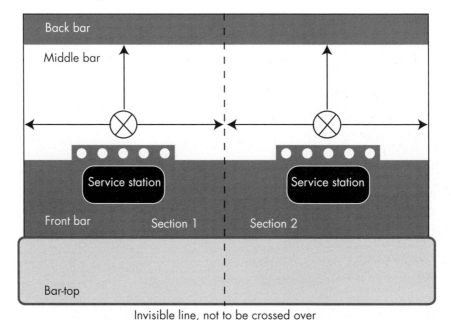

Invisible line, not to be crossed over
unless absolutely necessary

⊗ Bartender position

Using two hands

It helps for a bartender to be ambidextrous when preparing drinks. Imagine a line running straight through the centre of the ice well – dividing it into two parts. Everything on the left-hand side is picked up with the left hand and everything positioned on the right-hand side is accessed with the right hand.

A 'crossover' is when a bartender reaches with one hand over the other to pick something up. Doing this makes one hand ineffective and unable to perform a task, slowing the bartender down. If an item is positioned near one hand but needed by the opposite, it should be picked up by the hand closest and passed to the other hand.

> An exception to the principle of using two hands is layered drinks, which are easier to make holding the glass in one hand.

Recognising crossovers helps to promote efficient workflow by ensuring that the bartender does not block the full use of two hands when mixing.

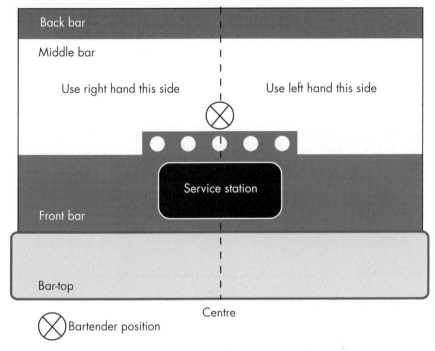

Centre

Bartender position

Usíng a buíldíng tray

Placing a mixed drink down on the building tray (or area) is a critical step to faster bar service. By letting go of the drink, the bartender is able to use both hands to make the drink, speeding up the rate at which it can be prepared. This is especially relevant to cocktails.

Glasses should be placed touching lip-to-lip on the building tray in the order that the bartender is going to mix them. Doing this saves space on the building tray and allows the bartender to run post-mix and juices over the top of two or more drinks without spillage, also contributing to a faster drink.

Usíng the team

Bar service is more effective if the full force of the team is harnessed. All staff should work together with the same objective: to provide excellent customer service. A simple example of teamwork is for an unoccupied bartender to take the money while another bartender prepares the drinks.

Bartenders should always be on the lookout for opportunities to give and receive help. If one bartender is closer to the fridge, it may be faster to ask that person to fetch an item from the fridge rather than the other bartender leaving the station.

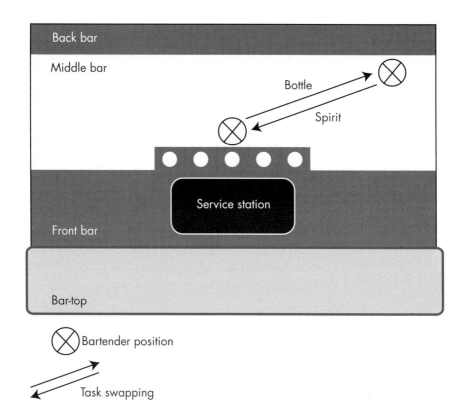

Thinking ahead

A bartender mixing drinks must always be asking: 'What is the next movement needed next in order to complete the drink?' By doing this, the bartender is able to think a step or two ahead of the job at hand. Once a movement is initiated, he or she should be thinking of the next move. For example, while a bartender is mixing a basic spirit, he or she may be thinking about the ingredients or equipment needed for the next drink.

Equipment holds

Glassware

Commonly used tumblers and highball glasses should be stacked upside down, as close as possible to the ice well. Glasses should be picked up from the base and never handled by the rim, unless they are being collected for washing. Avoid handling glasses around the top.

A bartender should be able to hold two or three rocks or spirit glasses in one hand, making sure that the lips of the glasses are as close together as possible. This will assist the bartender in 'icing down' the glasses (adding ice) in the minimum time (i.e. with one scoop).

Shakers

When using an American cocktail shaker, the bartender starts by adding ice to the mixing glass, then adding the ingredients. The mixing glass (or shaker top) is handled by the body for single cocktails and by the base when icing two at a time. Standard shakers are handled by the body, with a finger held over the lid.

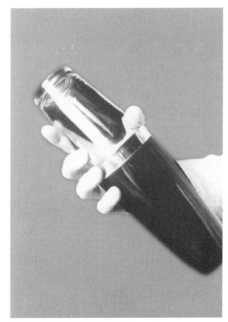

Blenders

Blenders without handles should be gripped around the body of the equipment. When adding ice to two blenders, the bartender should hold the two blenders together in one hand, holding them by the base.

The blender jug should be firmly fitted to the motor and the blender should be started with one hand holding the top in case it jumps off.

Bottles

Holding a bottle by the neck helps control the flow of alcohol into a vessel or glass. Spirit and liqueur bottles should be held with a firm grip around the neck of the bottle, with the index finger curved around the top of the free-pourer. (This prevents the pourer from falling off if loose.)

Keep finger away from air hole as this may block the flow of liquid.

Spirit measures

A spirit measure (jigger) is used to make an exact measurement of liquid poured from a bottle. The jigger is picked up at the same time as the bottle. Held between the thumb and index finger, the jigger should be positioned as close as possible to the glass, either to the side or above the glass.

When not in use, jiggers should be left upside down and draining, one on each side of the building tray. Some bartenders prefer to rinse jiggers between pours. This is really only necessary when moving from dark to white, or from liqueur to spirit.

The post-mix gun

The post-mix gun sits in a holster attached to either the front bar or bartop. To use the gun, a bartender removes it from its holster, gripping the body of the gun, and presses the appropriate soda button using the thumb or index finger. When finished with the gun, the bartender returns it to the holster, which is usually attached to the bar near the building tray.

Preparing basic spirits

Pouring

By law, a bartender must measure basic spirits in an approved jigger in front of the customer, ensuring consistency for the customer as well as accountability for the bartender. Bartenders should be able to pour a 30 mL shot confidently and quickly either with or without the jigger.

> The law requires bartenders to measure, or 'shot pour' the following spirits into a 30 mL measuring cup or jigger: whisky, vodka, gin, rum and brandy.

The shot-pour

The shot-pour is a 'must-know' skill. A bartender needs to be able to pour a level 30 mL shot in order to build mixed drinks quickly and confidently. Both hands should be used.

Steps for shot-pouring

▼ Using correct grips, bring bottle and jigger together over glass or shaker, tilting bottle 45–90 degrees, ensuring liquid is flowing out in a straight line and at the fastest possible rate.

▼ Cut off flow by lowering bottle and twisting pouring spout inwards over jigger to stop any drips. Replace bottle.

1

2

3

4

Practising shot-pouring builds up the skill of judging how much liquor is being poured, enabling the bartender to judge accurately a 30 mL free-pour.

The free-pour

The free-pour is probably the best known method of pouring. It involves the bartender pouring a 'guesstimate' amount of alcohol directly into a vessel, without using a measuring cup or jigger. By law, a bartender is only allowed to free-pour when using liqueurs, or adding spirits or liqueurs to a cocktail. Bartenders build reputations on their free-pours, priding themselves on both accuracy and showmanship.

When free-pouring into a glass on the building tray, the bartender has a hand free with which to add mixers.

Steps for free-pouring

- ▼ Pick up bottle, using correct grip and tilt to approximately 45–90 degrees, locking it up into curve of wrist and ensuring liquid is flowing out in a straight line and at the fastest possible rate.
- ▼ Cut off flow at desired measure by lowering bottle and twisting pouring spout inwards over vessel to stop any drips.

1

2

Sometimes bartenders are taught to 'count' when measuring a shot. For example, a 30 mL shot may be a count of three. It is recommended that bartenders first become competent at shot-pouring using a jigger, then using intuition and practice to judge a 30 mL or 60 mL shot.

The drag-pour

The drag-pour should only be used when mixing multiple liqueurs and/or cocktails. It should not be used with the five major spirit categories.

The drag-pour is a fairly recent arrival to Australia. It is a combination of a free-pour and a shot-pour, used when a bartender is busy. A jigger is used in line with government regulations, the difference being that the flow from the bottle is not 'cut off'. The bottle stays upright at a 45–90 degree angle while drinks are being poured, increasing the speed at which the drinks are prepared.

Drag-pouring is used when mixing multiple drinks, enabling the bartender to pour accurate shots in about half the time it takes to complete a standard shot-pour.

Steps for drag-pouring

▼ Pick up bottle, using correct grip, picking up jigger with opposite hand. Bring together over glass or shaker and tilt bottle 45–90 degrees, locking it up into curve of wrist and ensuring liquid is flowing out in a straight line and at a fast rate.

▼ When liquid in jigger reaches 20 mL (two-thirds full), it is dumped into vessel, with remaining 10 mL being free-poured.

▼ The jigger then catches flow of liquid again and is moved over to next glass to repeat the process. The last shot is fully measured. Replace bottle.

1

2

3

4

The drag-pour should be practised until the bartender is able to pour a shot accurately every time.

Spirit dispensers

Electronic spirit dispensers are fairly common in today's bars and provide an accurate and efficient means of dispensing house spirits. They are usually mounted above the service station but can also be positioned lower, near the bar-top.

Most dispensers use either 1.25-litre or 2-litre bottles, which last longer than a standard bottle during busy periods. Some dispensers draw from 20-litre containers stored in the cellar or nearby.

Electronic dispensers not only provide an accurate pouring system, but also now link with computerised stock control systems, enabling bar owners to monitor sales during the shift, and giving reports of what is selling.

Steps for using an electronic dispenser

▼ After adding ice, press glass on sensor pad below chosen spirit.
▼ Wait until full shot has been dispensed.
▼ Remove glass.

Some bartenders prefer to add the ice last as this reduces the risk of spillage.

Juices and milk

Juices should be stored in user-friendly containers to assisting pouring. Store-and-pour containers are ideal for this purpose. They are used much like bottles, although not as much care is needed with measuring and cutting the flow of liquid off.

Steps for pouring from a store-and-pour container

▼ Pick up container by the neck, bringing to a 45-degree angle over glass so it pours quickly.
▼ Cut off flow of juice by lowering container and twisting pouring spout inwards over glass to stop any drips.
▼ Replace container.

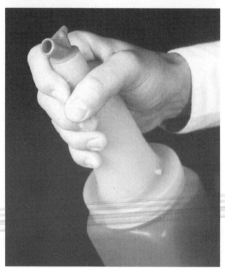

Adding ice

A large scoop or shaker can be used to scoop ice, enabling the bartender to scoop three to four glasses of ice in the one motion.

The scoop is kept in the ice, preferably dug in, ready for the next order. A right-handed bartender would pick up glasses with the left hand, while picking up the ice scoop with the right hand – bringing them together over the ice well to add the ice.

Efficiency tip

For single drink orders, the bartender would scoop only a small amount of ice, then add the ice to the glass over the ice well. For multiple drink orders, a bartender would scoop up a full scoop of ice, adding ice to 2–3 glasses at a time before placing them on the building tray.

Opening and serving wine

When a bottle of wine is ordered at the bar, the bottle is usually shown to the customer before opening in the same way as for table service to ensure that it is the right one.

Backup house red and white wine should be decorked prior to the commencement of service, with corks left half way in for easy removal. Since it is sometimes difficult to estimate how much wine will be consumed during a shift, a bartender sometimes has to open new bottles in mid-service.

The difference lies in the way the bartender opens the bottle. At the bar the cork may be removed in a faster manner. Some bars are fitted with a decorking device (rapid opener), which allows the bartender to quickly remove the cork by simply placing the neck of the bottle in the device and pulling the lever. This machine is best used for bottled house wine and is not appropriate for opening expensive wines, which should be opened at the table.

Still wine

A wine opener (waiter's friend) is commonly used to open wine bottles. It consists of a small knife, a lever and a corkscrew (see page 29). A waiter's cloth is optional and prevents drips.

Opening still wine

Opening a wine bottle should take no longer than 10–15 seconds for an experienced bartender.

▼ Show the label to the customer, confirming it is the right one.
▼ Prepare the wine opener by folding out the knife.

1

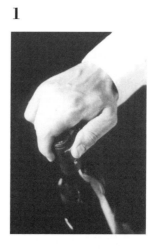

▼ Grip the neck of the bottle with the index finger over the top and the thumb pressing against the knife, locking it under the rim of the neck.

▼ Twist the base of the bottle in both directions to remove foil covering.

▼ Hold the corkscrew at a 90-degree angle to the cork, finding the centre of the cork with the point.

▼ Press the point in, lift and turn a full revolution to be in line with the cork, with the cork facing straight down.

▼ Twist the corkscrew in but leave one 'twist' out of the cork.

▼ Position the lever on the edge of the bottle, gripping the handle with one hand and around the neck and lever with the other.

▼ Gently pull the lever up, making sure the cork is not tearing. If it begins to break, stop the process, twist the corkscrew in another revolution and try again.

The steps to serving a bottle of wine to a customer are:

2

3

Serving still wine

▼ With the label facing towards the customer, wrap the wine cloth around the bottle (optional).

▼ Serve a small sample to the customer ordering the bottle.

▼ Upon approval, serve guests first and work back to the host. (The recommended serving size is about 100 mL.)

▼ Leave the bottle on the bar facing the customer or keep it on ice and top up glasses when necessary.

Sparkling wine

1

A tea towel or waiter's cloth is handy for opening sparkling wine quickly and cleanly.

Opening sparkling wine

▼ Remove the foil cover from around the neck.

▼ Pull the wire ringlet out and twist it until undone.

▼ Place one hand around the cork and the other around the base of the bottle.

A cloth is sometimes placed over the cork when opening to add friction and catch any spills.

86

▼ Grip the cork tightly through the cloth, levering it out on an angle while simultaneously rotating the bottom of the bottle.

▼ The cork should come out with a slight 'hiss', not a 'pop' (unless it is for effect).

Serving sparkling wine

▼ No taste test is needed.

▼ Place thumb into 'pitted' bottom of bottle, with other fingers around the base.

▼ Pour a small amount into each glass (glasses are best chilled).

▼ Top up each glass evenly (serving size is approximately 100 mL).

▼ Leave opened bottle in an ice bucket with a serving cloth draped over the top.

2

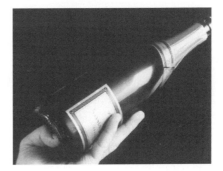

87

3

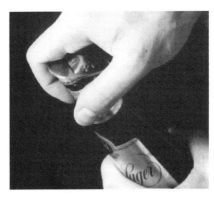

Opening and serving ready-to-drink products (RTDs)

There are three kinds of bottle caps used on RTDs – the pop-top, the twist-top and the screw-cap. The pop-top cannot be opened by hand alone – the latter two are possible to open by hand, although this is not recommended with the twist-top.

Many bottled beverages are now produced with the twist-top caps, allowing opening without a bottle opener – but be careful as twist-top caps are firmly secured and may tear a bartender's skin. It is always preferable to use a bottle opener when removing a twist-top cap.

Using a bottle opener

▼ Hold index finger over the top of the opener.

▼ Place it over the cap.

▼ Leverage it under part of the cap closest to you and pull up in a single firm motion.

Do not let caps fall to the ground – this is untidy and can cause accidents.

Efficiency tip

When a bartender is opening multiple pop-tops, all of the required beverages should be brought to the front bar (i.e. facing the customer) and opened. If a bartender is not equipped with an opener, he or she may have to either interrupt service to find one, or use an opener fixed to the bar.

The disadvantage of a fixed opener is that the bartender has to move to the opener rather than opening the bottles in one place near the customer – saving time and energy.

To use a fixed opener, lock the bottle in between the lugs and move the bottle downwards to remove the cap. The cap should ideally fall into a catcher underneath the opener – ensuring no caps end up on the floor.

Pouring draught beer

Pouring beer is one of the easier skills for a bartender to master. In larger venues, most of the hard work is done by the cellar person, who ensures that the kegs are connected and gassed correctly.

All that is left for the bartender to do is to open the beer taps to start the flow of beer and close the beer tap to stop the flow.

Kinds of beer taps

The two-position tap – This tap is 'off' when positioned up and 'on' when positioned down. It is spring loaded and can easily be flicked to the 'off' position to stop the flow of beer. There is no mid-way position on these taps, and with the beer inside the tap under pressure, it will froth up if the valve in the tap is left half opened.

The three-position tap – This tap has two 'off' positions to the left and right sides. The tap is only open when the tap is pointed towards the bartender (or at a 90-degree angle to the bar). Like the two-position tap, it is spring-loaded and is flicked back to either side to close off the flow.

The gun – Popular in large sporting venues, the beer gun uses a valve that is opened and closed by squeezing a trigger-style handle. It is spring-loaded to the 'off' position and will flick off as soon as the grip is released.

Pouring a beer

▼ Hold the nozzle of the tap near the inside edge of the glass (This helps to disperse the beer into the glass without letting it froth up too much.)

▼ Open tap quickly to 'on' position.

▼ Straighten glass slowly as beer rises.

▼ Some bartenders cut off the flow at about the half-way mark and wait for the bubbles/head to settle, then reposition the nozzle in the glass and straighten the glass as the beer fills – cutting off the flow to leave a head of approximately 1–2 cm. This is known as the two-pour method.

The other method involves only one stage (the one-pour method). The bartender keeps the flow going until the glass is nearly full, achieving the same result. Both methods are claimed to be the best!

1

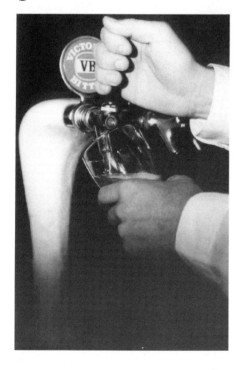

2

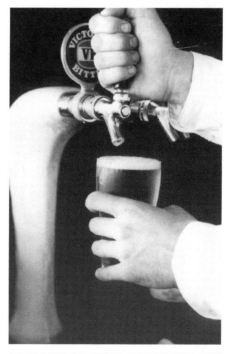

A little beer froth may flow over the side of the glass after pouring. If this is excessive, either the bartender is pouring incorrectly or the beer lines need maintenance.

Multiple beer pouring

Often a bartender will take an order for several glasses of the same beer. It is better to pour these together than one by one.

Multiple beer pouring

▼ Have one glass positioned under the tap and the remaining glasses nearby.

▼ Open the tap with free hand (i.e. hand not holding the glass). After opening the tap, move free hand to pick up the second glass.

▼ Drop the first beer away and catch the beer flow into the second glass that has just been picked up.

▼ Place first beer down on the bar and use free hand to close the tap.

▼ For two-pour beers, repeat the procedure.

1

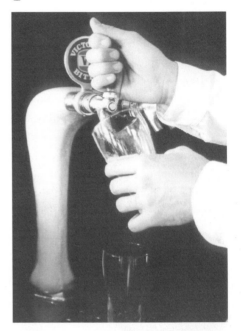

2

3

CHAPTER

Cocktails

Different occasions call for different cocktails.

The type of cocktail to prepare for a customer depends on a variety of factors, including the time of day, the venue, and, of course, taste preferences. People will tend to choose a drink that best complements the occasion (e.g. gin and tonic in hot weather).

Alcoholic drinks are generally served with meals in the evening. Cocktails lend themselves to some occasions when other alcoholic beverages may not be as appropriate or interesting, for example, when on holiday.

Examples of cocktail occasions

Occasion	Beverage
Morning	Bloody Mary
Afternoon	Screwdriver
Pre-dinner	Martini
After dinner	Mudslide
Celebration	B2
Hot weather	Mango daiquiri

Types of cocktails

To understand the types of cocktails, it is helpful to group them in categories with similar characteristics. This provides a framework to help choose the best cocktail for a particular occasion. There are six major categories.

1 Pre-dinner cocktails
2 Creamy cocktails
3 Long cocktails
4 Sour cocktails
5 Shot cocktails
6 Non-alcoholic cocktails

Pre-dinner cocktails

Pre-dinner cocktails are usually intended for consumption prior to eating. The intention is to stimulate the appetite and increase the enjoyment of the meal. The base spirit of a short cocktail is usually clear, but could be rye whisky or brandy. The characteristics of a pre-dinner cocktail are:

Potent	High alcohol content
Short	No more than three ingredients
Translucent	Not mixed with juice or cream

Other identifying factors for short cocktails are:

Glass	Less than 250 mL (e.g. small Martini, champagne, rocks)
Garnish	Single fruit garnish (e.g. olive, onion, twist or cherry)

The ingredients of a pre-dinner cocktail follow the general rule:

1 30–60 mL base spirit
2 15–30 mL added spirit/liqueur/flavouring
3 Colouring/garnish

Cocktails should generally not contain any more than 75 mL of alcohol.

Example of a pre-dinner cocktail

Martini

60 mL gin (base spirit)

5–15 mL dry vermouth (added spirit)

Olive (garnish)

For more information on cocktail recipes see page 123.

Creamy cocktails

Creamy cocktails are usually served after a meal. They contain cream and heavy mixers, sometimes giving them the quality of a dessert. The characteristics of a creamy cocktail are:

Sweet	Contains cream and sweet liqueurs
Full-bodied	Blended with ice and fruit
Satisfying	Dessert style

Other identifying factors of creamy cocktails are:

Glass	More than 250 mL (large Martini/large Hurricane)
Garnish	Elaborate garnishes and cocktail accessories (chocolate sauce, coconut sprinkles).

The ingredients of a creamy cocktail follow the general rule:

1 15–30 mL base spirit/liqueur
2 15–30 mL added spirit/liqueur
3 15–30 mL added liqueur
4 Fruit juice/fresh fruit (optional)
5 Cream, milk, and/or colouring

The base spirit/liqueur can be ambiguous in a creamy cocktail. Generally, a base spirit is not required in a creamy cocktail as it is lost in the mix with the cream.

Example of a creamy cocktail

Mudslide

20 mL vodka

20 mL Kahlua

20 mL Baileys

30 mL milk

30 mL cream

94

Long cocktails

Long cocktails are usually served in a long glass and can be served both during the day and at night. They consist mainly of fruit juice and sodas and are generally lower in alcohol content by volume than the other categories. They're also great for drinking by the pool! The characteristics of a long cocktail are:

Refreshing	Best consumed on a hot day
Icy	Built with lots of ice
Non-creamy	Light refreshing mixers used
Colourful	Vibrant colours sometimes used

Other identifying factors of long cocktails are:

Glass	More than 250 mL (Hurricane, Highball)
Garnish	Fresh fruit (e.g. orange, lemon, apple), parasols

The ingredients of a long cocktail follow the general rule:

1 30 mL base spirit

2 15–30 mL added spirit/liqueur

3 15–30 mL added liqueur

4 Fruit juice/soda

5 Fruit juice/colouring

The base spirit for a long cocktail is nearly always a white spirit as they are more suitable to mixing with sodas and juices.

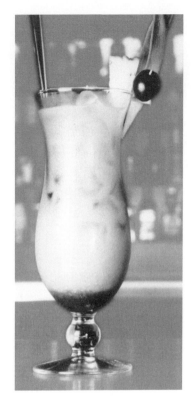

Example of a long cocktail

Mai Tai

30 mL white rum

15 mL dark rum

15 mL amaretto

15 mL triple sec

30 mL sweet and sour

30 mL pineapple juice

30 mL orange juice

Dash grenadine

Sour cocktails

Sour cocktails are a balanced combination of spirits and liqueurs, lime or lemon juice and sugar syrup. They are suitable for drinking on most occasions but are best consumed in the late afternoon or early evening.

The sour category is presently very popular in Australia, headed by cocktails such as Illusion, Margaritas and daiquiris. The characteristics of the sour cocktail are:

Sour	Contains lime or lemon juice, or Sour Mix (see page 96).
Non-creamy	Cream and lime or lemon juice don't mix

Other identifying factors of sour cocktails are:

Glass	(Large Martini, champagne flute)
Garnish	Single fruit garnish (lemon twist, cherry, lime circle)

The ingredients of a sour cocktail follow the general rule:

1 30–45 mL base spirit

2 15–30 mL added liqueur (optional)

3 Sour Mix (see page 96)

4 Fruit (optional)

The base spirits for sour cocktails are usually white, although they vary from liqueurs to dark spirits.

Example of a sour cocktail

Margarita
45 mL tequila (base spirit)
15 mL Cointreau or triple sec
(added liqueur)
30 mL Sour Mix (see below)

Sour Mix

Sour Mix is a mixture of lemon or lime juice, water and sugar. The sugar is first dissolved in hot water and then lemon or lime juice is added. The mix is right when a balance is found between the sweet and sour tastes.

The recipe for Sour Mix is:
2 cups sugar
1 cup hot water
1 cup fresh lemon juice (or to taste)
Egg white (optional)

Sour Mix eliminates the need for the bartender to have to balance the ingredients while mixing, and contributes to faster, better prepared cocktails.

Memory guide to popular sour cocktails

The table following provides a framework to remember a number of popular sour cocktail recipes. By using the common recipe, different ingredients can be substituted to create different cocktails.

Cocktail		Base spirit		Added liqueur		Sour Mix
Common recipe 45 mL base spirit 15 mL added liqueur 30 mL Sour Mix						
Margarita	=	Tequila	+	Triple sec	+	Sour Mix
Strawberry Margarita	=	Tequila	+	Strawberry liqueur	+	Sour Mix
Daiquiri (classic)	=	White rum	+	Triple sec	+	Sour Mix
Strawberry Daiquiri	=	White rum	+	Strawberry liqueur	+	Sour Mix
Banana Daiquiri	=	White rum	+	Banana liqueur	+	Sour Mix
Kamikaze	=	Vodka	+	Triple sec	+	Sour Mix
Illusion	=	Vodka and Midori	+	Triple sec	+	Sour Mix

Shot cocktails

Shot cocktails are often served as accompaniments to other beverages. They are usually layered, and served in 30 mL shot glasses, and can be sipped or 'shot'. Shot cocktails are often served to celebrate a special occasion and are mainly served later in the evening.

The characteristics of a shot cocktail are:

Small	30 mL or 60 mL shot glass
No ice	No space for ice
Coloured	Usually contain colourful liqueurs

A wide range of ingredients can be used in a shot cocktail. It is best to use compatible flavours, but there are really no rules.

In order to mix shot cocktails properly, a bartender must be familiar with the density of a spirits and liqueurs. Density is determined by sugar content. For example, Kahlua has a high sugar content and is heavier than a spirit such as vodka.

Guideline to follow when layering shot cocktails:

Lightest

Heaviest

Spirits (vodka, white rum, tequila)

Light liqueurs (Cointreau, Grand Marnier)

Cream liqueurs (Baileys)

Heavy liqueurs (Midori, sambuca, Tia Maria, peach schnapps)

Super sweet (grenadine, créme de cassis, Kahlua)

Example of a shot cocktail

B52
10 mL Kahlua
10 mL Baileys
10 mL Cointreau

Non-alcoholic cocktails

Non-alcoholic cocktails are sometimes known as 'mocktails', or virgin cocktails (classic cocktails that contain no alcohol). Although soda and juices satisfy much of the demand for non-alcoholic drinks, there are often requests for a bartender to create more interesting non-alcoholic concoctions.

As with cocktails, mocktails look and taste better than any of their individual components. For example, a virgin Pina Colada is much more exciting to the customer than a straight pineapple juice.

Non-alcoholic cocktails were typically a blend of different fruits and juices with sugar syrup used to provide sweetness. Now there is a large variety of non-alcoholic fruit syrups, not widely available in Australia until a few years ago, from the classical to the rare and exotic.

In this time of the responsible service of alcohol, bars and bartenders must be prepared to adapt their mixing styles to suit the changing marketplace.

Non-alcoholic cocktails are usually quite large and require a large cocktail glass.

Mixing methods

This section covers the practical skills required to create classic cocktails and mixed drinks. There are no standardised rules for mixing cocktails. The only limit to the creation of mixed drinks and cocktails is the bartender's imagination. Since no two cocktail books tell the same story, it is often left to the bartender to choose the best method to suit a particular drink or occasion.

Methods used to mix drinks include:

Build	Ingredients poured over ice
Shake	Ingredients shaken with ice
Blend	Ingredients blended with ice
Stir	Ingredients stirred over ice
Muddle	Ingredients crushed using a pestle
Layer	Ingredients layered one on the other (no ice)
Combination	Combination of methods

Build

A cocktail is built so that ingredients benefit from a slow dilution process (with ice melting into drink). This method in most commonly used when mixing basic spirits and sodas (e.g. bourbon and cola) and also for cocktails such as a Mai Tai.

Building a cocktail requires the following items:

- ✓ Ice
- ✓ Ice scoop
- ✓ Ingredients
- ✓ Pourers and measures
- ✓ Appropriate glassware
- ✓ Garnishes

Glassware for a mixed drink is normally 200–240 mL (e.g. rocks). Glassware for built cocktails is often larger, 360–450 mL (e.g. highball)

Steps for building

▼ Pick up glass and add ice.
▼ Place glass on building tray, pouring spirits and liqueurs over ice.
▼ Add mixers and garnish.

Spirits and liqueurs can legally be free-poured when used in a cocktail.
See page 81.

Shake

A cocktail is shaken when it is required to be completely chilled and mixed. Shaking cracks the ice and partly dilutes the contents of the shaker. This method is commonly used to mix heavy ingredients such as orange juice and cream. The method of shaking is often used for cocktails in the sour and creamy categories, e.g. Margarita and Golden Dream.

Shaking a cocktail requires the following items:

- ✓ Ice
- ✓ Ice scoop
- ✓ Ingredients
- ✓ Cocktail shaker
- ✓ Cocktail strainer (if using an American shaker)
- ✓ Pourers and measures
- ✓ Appropriate glassware
- ✓ Garnishes

Glassware for shaken mixed drinks would normally be a 300 mL or larger cocktail glass (e.g. 300 mL large Martini).

Steps for shaking

- ▼ Pick up shaker and add ice to mixing glass or shaker base.
- ▼ Place mixing glass or shaker on building tray. Add spirits, liqueurs and mixers.
- ▼ Put top on shaker and shake with lid of shaker facing over shoulder. Shake vigorously for 10 seconds, ensuring that ice hits top and bottom of shaker a number of times. (Condensation on shaker base indicates drink is ready.) Remove lid and place strainer over shaker base (if using American shaker) and pour gently into centre of glass.
- ▼ Garnish drink.

Blend

A cocktail is often blended when it contains fresh fruit or other heavy ingredients. This method is also used to crush ice into the drink – turning it slushy. Blending is most commonly used for cocktails in creamy and sour cocktail categories, for example Mudslide and Banana Daiquiri.

Blending a cocktail requires the following items:

- ✓ Ice
- ✓ Ice scoop
- ✓ Ingredients
- ✓ Cocktail blender
- ✓ Pourers and measures
- ✓ Appropriate glassware
- ✓ Garnishes

Glassware for blended mixed drinks would normally be larger than those used for the other methods, as the blended ice gives body to the drink (e.g. Hurricane).

Steps for blending

- ▼ Pick up blender and add ice.
- ▼ Place blender on building tray and add spirits, liqueurs and mixers.
- ▼ Place lid on blender and turn it on, blending for 20–30 seconds or until mixture is smooth (it is usually ready when ice cannot be heard rattling in blender). Garnish glass while blending.
- ▼ Turn off blender.
- ▼ Gently strain or pour mixture into centre of garnished glass.

It is advisable to hold the lid securely on for the first few seconds so that it does not come loose.

Stir

Stirring is most commonly used for cocktails when a chill is required throughout the mixture. It is most commonly used when mixing pre-dinner drinks such as Martinis or Manhattans, and is also useful for chilling a spirit without diluting it too much (e.g. vodka).

Stirring a mixed drink requires the following items:

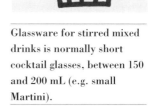

✓ Ice	✓ Cocktail strainer
✓ Ice scoop	✓ Pourers and measures
✓ Ingredients	✓ Appropriate glassware
✓ Mixing glass	✓ Garnish
✓ Mixing spoon	

Glassware for stirred mixed drinks is normally short cocktail glasses, between 150 and 200 mL (e.g. small Martini).

101

Steps for stirring

▼ Pick up mixing glass and add ice (also add ice to glass to chill it).

▼ Place both glasses on building tray and pour spirits, liqueurs and mixers (if any) into mixing glass.

▼ Stir liquid in mixing glass by rotating spoon around edge of glass a few times – trying not to crack or melt the ice. The back of the spoon is turned towards the glass.

▼ Place strainer on top of mixing glass and pour gently into centre of chilled glass.

▼ Garnish.

Muddle

A cocktail is muddled when one or more of the ingredients needs to be crushed into the drink. It is commonly used to mix granulated sugar with fresh fruits and herbs (such as mint) and helps to extract the flavours from them. Examples include Mojito and Caipiroska.

Muddling a cocktail requires the following equipment:

✓ Ingredients
✓ Appropriate glassware (usually rocks or highball)
✓ Pestle

Steps for muddling

▼ Add ingredients to glassware.

▼ Crush sugar and fruit by pressing pestle firmly downwards and twisting clockwise.

▼ Repeat until ingredients are thoroughly mixed.

▼ Add ice and other ingredients.

It is common to shake the cocktail after using the pestle to ensure consistent flavour throughout the cocktail.

Layer

A mixed drink is layered to create a contrasting colour effect. This method is most commonly used when making shot cocktails such as B52 and Slippery Nipple.

Layering a cocktail requires the following items:

- ✓ Ingredients
- ✓ Bar spoon (optional)
- ✓ Pourers and measures
- ✓ Appropriate glassware

Glassware for layered mixed drinks is normally a 30 mL or 60 mL shot glass.

Steps for layering

▼ Pick up shot glass and place on bar-top.

▼ Place mixing spoon upside down into glass and pour ingredients over back of spoon, gently raising spoon as glass fills.

▼ Repeat if necessary.

Note: In speed bars the mixing spoon is normally not used. A pourer, if used correctly, can act as a liquid diffuser and can effectively layer as well as a mixing spoon. This involves the glass being tilted towards the pourer and the bottle being gently manoeuvred into the glass. This method should be only be used after perfecting layering with a mixing spoon.

Combination

Combining two mixing methods can create an interesting effect. Although it may not be as time-efficient as using a single method, the combination of mixing methods has won cocktail competitions because of originality and style.

A common combination of mixing methods is to layer a shaken combination of ingredients on a blended mixture of ingredients.

Other combinations include:

▼ Layer blended over shaken mixture
▼ Layer blended over built mixture

Garnishing

The garnish is an important part of the finished drink. Some mixed drinks are instantly recognisable by the garnish (e.g. the olive in a Martini or the pineapple on a Pina Colada).

An attractive garnish might do just as much to sell a drink as bartender recommendation, as customers are often influenced simply by the appearance of the cocktail.

Although the garnishes for some cocktails classics never change, there is a trend towards less garnish and more cocktail, giving customers better value for money.

Below are some factors to consider when preparing a garnish for a cocktail.

Colour

The colour of the garnish should be compatible or provide a contrast to the colour of the drink. For example, a pink coloured drink benefits from a red cherry and a blue drink is brought to life with a yellow slice of pineapple.

Taste

If an edible garnish is used, it should be compatible with one or more of the ingredients in the cocktail. For example, a cocktail containing pineapple juice would benefit from a pineapple slice and a cocktail containing lemon juice would be complemented by a lemon slice.

Size

The size of a garnish should be appropriate for the size of the glass. For example, a mixed drink in a small glass may benefit from a small cherry, but not a large orange slice.

Shape

The shape of the glass helps determine the best garnish to use for it. For example, lime circles may complement a large Martini glass, but a pineapple segment may not, as it is at odds with the shape of the glass.

Name

The name of a particular mixed drink often provides hints as to the garnish to use with it. For example, a banana slice might be used with a Banana Daiquiri.

Garnish placement

Garnishes can be used as follows:

Mounted   Placed on the side of a glass (e.g. lime circle in Margarita)
Floated   Floated in the mixture (e.g. lemon slice in vodka and lemonade)
Sunk   Dropped into the bottom of the glass (e.g. cherry in Manhattan)

Different methods are used for different effects. The most common garnishing method used in basic drinks is floating, giving life to the drink through adding a piece of fruit on top of the ice. A selection of cut fruit may be floated on the top of a mixed drink to give it a tropical effect and add flavour.

Garnishes are normally floated for normal mixed spirits, and mounted or sunk for cocktails.

Cocktail recipe writing

If you intend to create your own cocktails or to record the cocktails available in the bar, they should be recorded accurately. An index of available cocktails allows preparation of a wider range of cocktails than traditional favourites and house specials. The elements that should be covered when documenting cocktail recipes are:

1 Name (listed in alphabetical order).

2 Ingredients measured in mL (in order of use).

3 Mixing method (build, shake, blend, stir, layer, float, combination).

4 Glass should be specified and/or pictured (e.g. highball, small Martini).

5 Garnish should be specified and/or pictured (e.g. pineapple flower, mounted cherry).

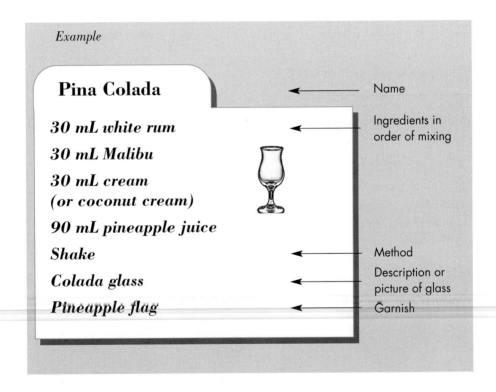

Example

Pina Colada ← Name

30 mL white rum ← Ingredients in order of mixing

30 mL Malibu

30 mL cream (or coconut cream)

90 mL pineapple juice

Shake ← Method

Colada glass ← Description or picture of glass

Pineapple flag ← Garnish

Preparing cocktail lists

A cocktail list should feature a variety of cocktail types and a variety of different mixing methods. Too many cocktails on the list makes choosing a cocktail difficult.

Preparing a cocktail list

1 Find out what the regular customers enjoy drinking.

2 Compile a basic list, including suggestions from other bartenders.

3 Include some classic cocktails for drinkers with a preference for traditional cocktails.

4 Cull the list down to a maximum of 10–15 cocktails.

5 The revised list (assuming 10 cocktails) could include a variety of categories, for example:
   - Creamy cocktails (2)
   - Pre-dinner cocktails (1)
   - Sour cocktails (2)
   - Long cocktails (2)
   - Shot cocktails (2)
   - Non-alcoholic cocktails (1)

Consideration should also be given to seasonality. For example, summer could see more long and sour cocktails being featured. Likewise, in winter more creamy and hot drinks could be featured.

CHAPTER **11**

Product and equipment placement

Product and equipment placement dictates service speed.

The modern bar pays particular attention to the positioning of products and equipment. If the ingredients for a cocktail or mixed drink are not close at hand, a drink may take longer to prepare. If a particular drink or cocktail is popular, a lot of time may be wasted as the bartender has to move away from the serving area to fetch the equipment and/or ingredients.

Products should be positioned in a bar according to the following criteria:

Demand	The more a product is used, the closer it should be.
Grouping categories	Similar products should be positioned together, making finding them a lot easier.
Aesthetics	The products should look good once they are in place.

When setting up a bar from scratch, it may be difficult to predict what the most popular products will be and where the best place is for them. It is necessary to make a judgement about the initial product placement, then make adjustments to it over time. A compromise will often be necessary to get the right balance for a particular bar.

Begin by placing the most popular products at the service station, and finish at the back bar with the slowest moving lines. Likewise, bottled beer and ready-to-drink beverages such as wine coolers are positioned in fridges according to their popularity.

109

Product placement

Each service station should have a full range of house spirits in the speed rack including bourbon, Scotch, vodka, gin, rum and tequila. These spirits should be ranged in order from the most frequently ordered spirit closest at hand to the least frequently ordered spirit furthest away.

Products are generally positioned from right to left, as most bartenders are right handed.

If bourbon is the most popular spirit in a venue, it should be placed closest to the bartender for easy reach. If Scotch is the second most popular spirit, it should appear next, and so on.

Commonly asked-for proprietary brands (e.g. Johnnie Walker Red, Bundaberg rum) are also sometimes included in the speed rack because customers often ask for them specifically rather than a house spirit. These popular 'mid shelf' (or more expensive) spirits are best positioned close to the house spirits.

Top-shelf (most expensive) spirits (e.g. cognac) are seldom found in or around the service well as they are used less frequently than their cheaper counterparts.

Back bar products

The back bar is the area used to showcase the bar's products and should be aesthetically pleasing as well as functional. The back bar is home to the majority of the bar's spirits and liqueurs and careful thought should be given to their arrangement. Spirits such as Wild Turkey and Absolut, while not as popular as their cheaper counterparts, should be positioned fairly close to the bartender, as they are often responsible for their fair share of sales. As a product's popularity over time increases or decreases, it can be repositioned accordingly.

Colourful liqueurs help to bring the back bar to life if prominently displayed. Generic liqueur ranges such as Vok or Seagram are often lined up, showcasing their colours. Commonly used liqueurs such as blue curaçao and crème de cacao may be closer to service points, whereas less commonly used liqueurs such as advocaat and cherry brandy may be positioned further away. Proprietary liqueurs such as

Cointreau, Tia Maria and Frangelico may be grouped, making it easier for the bartender to find them.

A good way to look at back bar product placement is to think through the most common cocktails and beverages that the bar is expected to serve and endeavour to position the main ingredients so that the bartender does not have to move too far to fetch them.

Fridges

Bottled beer and ready-to-drink beverages (RTDs) need to be served cold, either from ice or straight from the fridge. If a particular RTD is popular (e.g. Stoli Ruski), it needs to be placed in a convenient location, such as on the top shelf of the fridge.

Some bars have walk-in coolrooms, enabling the RTDs to be continually restocked without disruption to service.

Refrigeration is often located at the back bar, forcing the bartender to leave the service station in order to complete the order. Some bars have overcome this problem by bringing the most popular RTDs forward to the front bar

A common solution is the use of free-standing ice bins. It is not uncommon to have a number of backup bins at the back of house, ready to be iced down when the bins behind the bar run out. This method is effective in keeping drinks cold and permanently on hand.

Condiments

Condiments include a variety of non-alcoholic ingredients. Depending on the range of drinks on offer, they may or may not be used frequently.

Condiments should be ideally be kept on the front bar near the service station. They are usually kept together in a caddy and should include:

Salt and pepper
Nutmeg
Cinnamon
Tabasco
Worcestershire sauce
Chocolate sauce

Front bar equipment

Often a simple repositioning of equipment can achieve a marked improvement in productivity. Blenders, shakers and cutting boards and even the register can be tried in different places. Experimentation can help determine the optimum position for equipment.

Bar equipment should normally be centred around the ice well, with the bartender not having to move more than one step in any direction. To have to move further than this (except to take orders) means efficiency is lost.

Questions to ask when positioning or repositioning equipment include:

▼ What are the bar's most popular drinks?
▼ What equipment is needed in order to prepare these drinks?
▼ Where would be the most convenient location from which to access this equipment?
▼ Where else can it be positioned as a contingency?

Bar equipment placement

Ice blender	Beside ice well
Cocktail shaker	In or around ice well or upside down on building tray
Strainer	Near or beside shaker tin/glass
Bar spoon	Near mixing glass and cocktail equipment at back of ice well
Ice scoop	In ice well
Wine/bottle opener	On person or next to register
Salt rimmer	On bar-top or near cocktail glasses
Jigger/measuring cup	On side of building tray
Garnish tray	Next to building tray
Cutting board	Beside ice well – near blender
Fruit knife	Near cutting board
Free-pourers	In bottles – spares close at hand
Change plate	Near or on register
Store-and-pour containers	In ice well or speed rack
Register	Near service station

113

Glassware

Glassware can be divided into two categories:

1 Frequently used glasses (e.g. spirit and soft drink glasses)
2 Less frequently used glasses (e.g. large Martini and balloon glasses)

Frequently used glassware should be racked/stacked upside down on the front bar, within the bartender's reach, reducing the time it takes to make popular drinks. If stacked without using trays, the glassware should be placed on aerating mats so that bacteria or condensation cannot build up in glasses.

Less frequently used glasses are generally positioned on the back bar as they are called upon less often. They should be well polished before being put away.

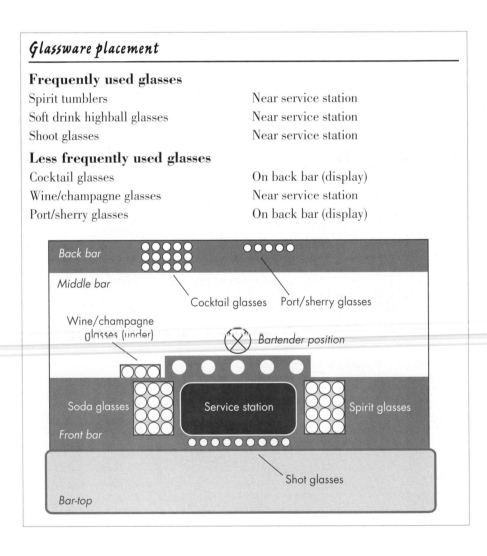

Glassware placement

Frequently used glasses

Spirit tumblers	Near service station
Soft drink highball glasses	Near service station
Shoot glasses	Near service station

Less frequently used glasses

Cocktail glasses	On back bar (display)
Wine/champagne glasses	Near service station
Port/sherry glasses	On back bar (display)

CHAPTER 12

Multiple drink mixing

A bartender should always prepare more than three drinks at a time in a busy bar.

Experienced bartenders have learned by trial and error the secrets of how to prepare multiple drink orders in the minimum amount of time.

Multiple drink mixing requires a thorough knowledge of products and bar layout. A bartender who is new to a bar will not know where all products and equipment are positioned and will be unable to establish an efficient workflow until better knowledge is gained.

By planning the order in which drinks are made, a bartender is able to prepare up to 10 or more drinks at a time, keeping on top of orders and working at optimum capacity. A bartender lacking the knowledge of drink prioritisation will generally prepare drinks as they are ordered – not understanding that the order in which the drinks are prepared makes a significant difference to their service speed.

Grouping of drinks

It is common practice for customers to group similar drinks together when ordering a round of drinks, thereby making them easier to remember. For example, a customer might order two bourbon and colas and a bottled beer – grouping the two spirits. Likewise, bartenders can group similar drinks together when preparing them in order to reduce preparation time. This can be applied to both large individual orders as well as combined orders.

Example

A bartender takes an order from one customer for a bourbon/cola. Another order is added on for a vodka/orange and another bourbon/cola.

The order is then remembered and prepared as: $2 \times$ bourbon/cola and $1 \times$ vodka/orange.

Order taken   Order rearranged

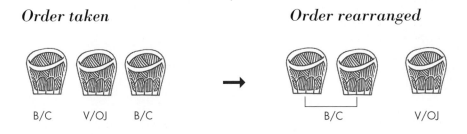

B/C   V/OJ   B/C   B/C   V/OJ

Some drinks require the bartender to move from the service station in order to prepare or fetch them. It is important that similar items within the order are prepared and/or fetched simultaneously, keeping movement away from the service station to a minimum.

Example

A bartender takes an order from a customer for a bottled beer, bourbon/cola and a vodka/orange. An additional order is added on for another bourbon/cola and bottled beer.

The order is then remembered and prepared as: $2 \times$ bourbon/cola, $1 \times$ vodka/orange, $2 \times$ bottled beer.

Order taken   Order rearranged

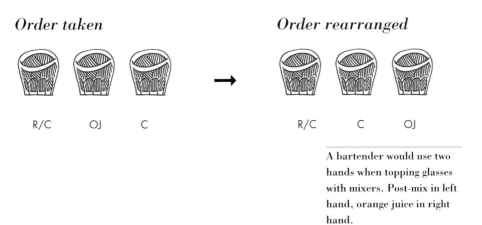

beer   B/C   V/O   B/C   beer   B/C   V/O   beer

Drinks with similar mixers should also be grouped as this enables the bartender to 'sweep' the mixers over the glasses – improving service speed.

Example

A bartender takes an order for a rum/cola and an orange juice. Another order for a plain cola is added on.

The order is then remembered and mixed as: $1 \times$ rum/cola, $1 \times$ cola and $1 \times$ orange juice.

Order taken   Order rearranged

R/C   OJ   C   R/C   C   OJ

A bartender would use two hands when topping glasses with mixers. Post-mix in left hand, orange juice in right hand.

Which cocktail first?

Bartenders often receive orders for a number of cocktails that require different preparation methods. By understanding the order in which methods should be used, a bartender can prioritise the cocktails into the most efficient sequence. It is best to plan preparation of cocktails according to the time it takes to prepare them, with the most time-consuming drinks made first.

118

Order for preparing multiple drinks

1st Blend   2nd Build   3rd Shake/Stir   4th Layer

Rearranging the order – examples

Example 1

A bartender takes the following order: B52 (layered), Golden Dream (shaken), Frozen Margarita (blended).

The drink order is rearranged to: Frozen Margarita, Golden Dream, B52.

Order taken   *Order rearranged*

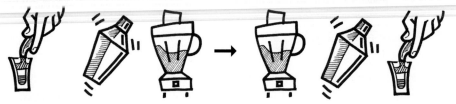

Step-by-step

▼ Pick up blender and shaker glass
▼ Add ice to both
▼ Line up on building tray or bench

▼ Pour Margarita ingredients
▼ BLEND Margarita
▼ Pour Golden Dream ingredients/salt rim glass
▼ SHAKE Golden Dream
▼ Turn blender off and pour Margarita into salt-rimmed glass
▼ Pour shaken cocktail
▼ Pick up shot glass
▼ LAYER B52
▼ Straw, garnish and serve all drinks

For more information on cocktail recipes, see Cocktail Recipes (page 123).

Example 2

A bartender takes the following order: Long Island Iced Tea (built), Kamikaze (shaken), Strawberry Daiquiri (blended).

The drink order is then rearranged to: Strawberry Daiquiri, Long Island Iced Tea, Kamikaze.

Order taken   *Order rearranged*

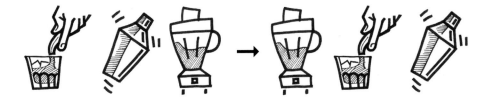

Step-by-step
▼ Pick up blender, shaker glass and tall cocktail glass
▼ Add ice to all
▼ Line up on building tray
▼ Pour Strawberry Daiquiri ingredients
▼ BLEND Daiquiri
▼ Pour Kamikaze ingredients
▼ Pour Long Island Iced Tea ingredients
▼ SHAKE Kamikaze/fetch glass
▼ Turn blender off and pour Daiquiri
▼ Pour Kamikaze
▼ Pick up shot glass
▼ LAYER B52
▼ Straw, garnish and serve all drinks

The positioning of equipment and products should allow maximum efficiency in production. If the post-mix gun is positioned on the right-hand side of the building tray, drinks with sodas should be prepared together on the right-hand side – affecting the order in which drinks are produced.

Preparing multiple orders

If a wide variety of drinks is ordered on a regular basis, the bartender needs to prioritise the drinks to plan the most efficient order in which to make them.

A bartender should be on the lookout for cocktails with similar ingredients and try to pour all measures required before replacing each bottle.

The following section introduces an American bartending system known as 'call order'. This provides guidelines to follow when preparing multiple drinks – helping a bartender to determine the most efficient sequence for making the drinks.

1 Blended cocktails/draught beer if two-pour

2 Basic spirits and liqueurs

3 Built cocktails

4 Shaken cocktails

5 Sodas and juices

6 Glasses of wine/draught beer

7 Bottled beer/RTDs

8 Layered shots

9 Hot drinks

The rule of thumb is that drinks that need to be blended or settled are prepared first (e.g. fruit daiquiris). Drinks that are prepared quickly or that take little effort to prepare are made last (e.g. bottled beer).

'Call order' came about by cocktail servers calling drink orders to bartenders, which over time became a system whereby the drinks were 'called in' in the fastest order in which to prepare them.

A full call order is not applicable in all bars as not all bars are designed or equipped to mix a full range of beverages. This example is a guideline for mixing a full range of drinks efficiently in an ideal environment.

Rearranging the order — examples

Example 1

A bartender takes the following combined order: 1 × bottled beer, 1 × vodka/orange juice, 1 × bourbon/cola and 1 × glass of wine.

The order is then rearranged to: 1 × bourbon/cola, 1 × vodka/orange juice, 1 × glass of wine, 1 × bottled beer.

Order taken   *Order rearranged*

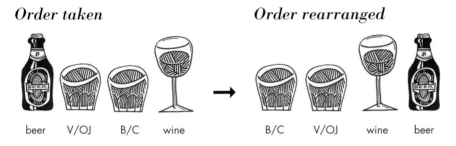

beer   V/OJ   B/C   wine   B/C   V/OJ   wine   beer

Step-by-step

- ▼ Pick up 2 rocks glasses
- ▼ Add ice to both
- ▼ Line up on building tray
- ▼ Pour bourbon then vodka
- ▼ Add cola and orange juice (using two hands)
- ▼ Straw and garnish
- ▼ Fetch wine glass and bottled beer
- ▼ Fill wine
- ▼ Open bottled beer

Efficiency tip

A bartender might call the bottled beer and/or wine away to a colleague to prepare, saving some time. A bartender might also ask a colleague to prepare the glass of wine while he or she mixes the spirits, increasing the service speed.

Example 2

A bartender takes the following combined order: 1 × shaker of Illusion, 1 × vodka/tonic, 1 × bourbon/cola, 1 × bottled beer.

The order is then rearranged to: 1 × bourbon/cola, 1 × vodka/tonic, 1 × shaker of Illusion, 1 × bottled beer.

Order taken   *Order rearranged*

shaker   V/T   B/C   beer   B/C   V/T   shaker   beer

Step by step

▼ Pick up 2 rocks glasses and shaker
▼ Add ice to all
▼ Line up on building tray
▼ Pour bourbon then vodka
▼ Pour Illusion ingredients
▼ Add sodas, and juices simultaneously
▼ SHAKE and pour
▼ Straw and garnish
▼ Fetch and open bottled beer
▼ Serve all drinks

Call order summary chart

Mix	Description	Category	Examples
1st	Time-consuming drinks	Blended drinks Draught beer	Frozen Margarita, Mudslide VB, Swan
2nd	Other iced drinks	Built drinks Shaken drinks Stirred drinks	Bourbon/Coke, orange juice Golden Dream, Whiskey Sour Martini
3rd	RTDs	Ready to drink	Stoli Ruski Heineken
4th	Hot drinks		Coffee Tea

Cocktail recipes

The following cocktail recipes have been selected from the most popular cocktails and mixed drinks found in bars and clubs. The recipes are arranged alphabetically with ingredients in order of use. The style of glass is pictured for convenience. Non-alcoholic cocktails and coffee drinks are separately listed.

The following measurements and terminology are used:

45mL	(1½ nips/fl oz)	**Top**	Fill glass
30mL	(1 nip/fl oz)	**Splash**	Approximately 10 mL
20mL	(⅓ nip/fl oz)	**Dash**	Approximately 5 mL
15mL	(½ nip/fl oz)	**Drop**	Approximately 1 mL

The ingredients and measures are indicative of what is being used in some of the most successful bars in the trade today. They differ in some respects from recipes in other books but are true to the origins of the drink and are appropriate for use all types of bars.

> As a general rule no cocktail has more than 75 mL of liquor in it.

From the dry Martini to Sex on the Beach and beyond, take your time to learn and practise the basics before moving on to mixing your own concoctions!

Key

Brandy balloon   Champagne   Colada

Highball   Hurricane   Large Martini

Small Martini   Rocks   Shot

Special coffee   Wine   Coupette

Alabama Slammer

30 mL vodka
15 mL Southern Comfort
15 mL sloe gin
10 mL amaretto
90 mL pineapple juice

Shake all ingredients with ice. Strain over cubed ice and garnish with lime wedge and cherry.

B52

10 mL Kahlua
10 mL Baileys
10 mL Cointreau

Layer in order listed.

Baybreeze

30 mL vodka
60 mL pineapple juice
60 mL cranberry juice

Build all ingredients over ice and garnish with lime wedge.

Bellini

30 mL puréed peaches
15 mL peach schnapps
Champagne

Mix peach schnapps and peach purée in glass and top with champagne.

Between the Sheets

20 mL brandy
20 mL triple sec
20 mL white rum
30 mL Sour Mix

[small]

Shake all ingredients with ice and strain. Garnish with lemon twist.

Black Russian

30 mL vodka
30 mL Kahlua
Cola (optional)

Build ingredients over ice.

Blood Clot

15 mL peach schnapps
15 mL Baileys
2 drops grenadine

Layer ingredients in order listed.

Bloody Mary

45 mL vodka
2 drops Tabasco
Dash Worcestershire Sauce
Dash lemon juice
Salt and pepper
Top with tomato juice

Shake all ingredients and strain over cubed ice. Garnish with celery stick.

Blue Lagoon

30 mL vodka
15 mL blue curaçao
30 mL Sour Mix
Top with lemonade

Shake first three ingredients then strain over ice and top with lemonade.

Brain

15 mL peach schnapps
15 mL vodka
4 drops Baileys

Layer vodka over peach schnapps then carefully add drops of Baileys to centre of glass.

Brain Haemorrhage

15 mL peach schnapps
15 mL vodka
4 drops Baileys
2 drops grenadine

Layer vodka over peach schnapps then carefully add drops of Baileys to centre of glass, followed by grenadine.

Brandy Alexander

30 mL brandy
30 mL crème de cacao
30 mL cream

[small]

Shake all ingredients with ice and strain. Cross two straws over glass and sprinkle with nutmeg. Remove straws.

Brave Bull

30 mL tequila
30 mL Kahlua

Build ingredients over ice and garnish with a lemon twist.

Brown Cow

30 mL Kahlua
Top with milk

Build ingredients over ice.

Bubblegum

30 mL Southern Comfort
30 mL banana liqueur
20 mL cream
Dash grenadine

Shake ingredients with ice and strain. Garnish with mounted cherry.

Caipiroska

45 mL vodka
15 mL sugar syrup
1 tsp sugar
1 fresh lime (cut into wedges)

Muddle sugar and lime then add vodka and shake. Pour over ice.

Cape Cod

30 mL vodka
Top with cranberry juice

Build ingredients over ice. Garnish with lime wedge.

Cow Puncher

30 mL white rum
30 mL crème de cacao
Top with milk

Build all ingredients over ice. Garnish with a cherry.

Cowboy

15 mL butterscotch schnapps
15 mL Baileys

Layer ingredients in order listed.

Cranberry Cooler

30 mL vodka
60 mL cranberry juice
15 mL sugar syrup
Top with soda

Build ingredients over ice and top with soda. Garnish with lime wedge.

Cranberry Kir

15 mL crème de cassis
30 mL cranberry juice
Top with chilled white wine

Add crème de cassis to glass then top with chilled cranberry juice
and white wine.

Cuba Libre

30 mL white rum
Top with cola
Dash of lime juice

Build ingredients over ice. Garnish with squeeze of fresh lime.

Daiquiri – Fruit

30 mL white rum
30 mL triple sec or fruit liqueur
30 mL Sour Mix
Fresh fruit

Blend all ingredients until smooth. Garnish with fruit slice.

Daiquiri – Original

45 mL white rum
15 mL triple sec or fruit liqueur
30 mL Sour Mix

Shake ingredients with ice and strain. Garnish with lime wheel.

[small]

57 T-Bird with California Plates

30 mL white rum
15 mL amaretto
15 mL sloe gin
90 mL orange juice
15 mL Grand Marnier (float)

Shake first four ingredients and strain. Float Grand Marnier and garnish with orange slice and cherry.

Freddy Fudpucker

30 mL tequila
120 mL orange juice
15 mL Galliano (float)

Build ingredients over ice. Garnish with orange slice and cherry.

French 75

15 mL gin
30 mL Sour Mix
Champagne

Shake first two ingredients and strain into glass. Top with champagne and garnish with lemon twist and cherry.

Fruit Tingle

30 mL blue curaçao
30 mL melon liqueur
Top with lemonade
Add dash of grenadine

Build first two ingredients over ice then top with lemonade. Add grenadine last and garnish with cherry.

Godmother

30 mL vodka
30 mL amaretto

Build ingredients over ice and garnish with two cherries.

Golden Cadillac

30 mL Galliano
30 mL crème de cacao (white)
30 mL cream

[small]

Shake all ingredients with ice and strain into glass.
Garnish with sprinkle of nutmeg and a cherry.

Golden Dream

30 mL Galliano
30 mL triple sec
30 mL cream
30 mL orange juice

[large]

Shake ingredients with ice and strain into glass.
Garnish with orange slice and cherry.

Grasshopper

30 mL crème de menthe (green)
30 mL crème de cacao (white)
30 mL cream

[small]

Shake ingredients with ice and strain into glass.
Garnish with two cherries.

Greyhound

30 mL vodka
Top with grapefruit juice

Build ingredients over ice.

Harvey Wallbanger

30 mL vodka
Top with orange juice
15 mL Galliano (float)

Build ingredients over ice (float Galliano last).
Garnish with orange slice and cherry.

Illusion

20 mL vodka
20 mL Midori
20 mL triple sec
30 mL lemon juice
Dash of lime cordial

[small]

Shake ingredients and strain into glass. Garnish with lime wheel. (To mix a
shaker of Illusion triple ingredients.) Pineapple juice is also often added.

Japanese Slipper

30 mL Midori
30 mL triple sec
30 mL lemon juice

[small]

Shake ingredients with ice and strain into glass.
Garnish with lime wheel and cherry.

Jelly Bean

45 mL ouzo
Dash grenadine
Top with lemonade

Add first two ingredients then top with lemonade.

Kamikaze

30 mL vodka
30 mL triple sec
30 mL lemon/lime juice
Dash of lime cordial

[small]

Shake ingredients with ice and strain into glass. Garnish with lime wheel.

Kir

15 mL crème de cassis
Top with chilled white wine

Add crème de cassis to glass and top with wine.

Kir Royale

15 mL crème de cassis
Top with champagne/sparkling wine

Add crème de cassis to glass and top with champagne or sparkling wine.
Garnish by dropping cherry into glass.

134

Long Beach Iced Tea

15 mL vodka
15 mL white rum
15 mL tequila
15 mL gin
15 mL triple sec
90 mL cranberry juice
30 mL Sour Mix

Build ingredients over ice and garnish with lime wedge.

Long Island Iced Tea

15 mL vodka
15 mL white rum
15 mL gin
15 mL tequila
15 mL triple sec
30 mL Sour Mix
Splash of cola

Build ingredients over ice and garnish with lemon slice.

Long Sloe Comfortable Screw up against the Wall

30 mL vodka
15 mL Southern Comfort
15 mL sloe gin
Top with orange juice
15 mL Galliano (float)

Build ingredients over ice. Garnish with orange slice and cherry.

Madras

30 mL vodka
60 mL cranberry juice
60 mL orange Juice

Build ingredients over ice. Garnish with lime wedge.

Mai Tai

30 mL white rum
15 mL dark rum
15 mL triple sec
15 mL amaretto
30 mL Sour Mix
30 mL pineapple juice
30 mL orange juice
Dash grenadine

Build ingredients over ice (add grenadine last).
Garnish with pineapple flag.

Manhattan

60 mL rye whiskey
10 mL sweet vermouth
2 drops Angostura Bitters

Shake ingredients with ice and strain. Garnish with cherry.

[small]

Margarita, Original

45 mL tequila
15 mL triple sec
30 mL Sour Mix

Shake all ingredients with ice and strain into salt-rimmed glass. Garnish with
lime circle. (Frozen = Blended)

[small]

Margarita, Fruit

40 mL tequila
15 mL triple sec or fruit liqueur
30 mL Sour Mix
Fresh fruit

Blend all ingredients with ice. Garnish with appropriate fruit slice.

Martini – Dry

60 mL gin
5 mL dry vermouth

Stir ingredients over ice and strain. Garnish with olive or lemon twist.   [small]

A Sweet Martini replaces dry vermouth with 10 mL of sweet
(rosso) vermouth.

Melon Ball

30 mL vodka
30 mL melon liqueur
Top with orange juice

Build ingredients over ice and garnish with cherry.

Mimosa

Half orange juice
Half champagne

Pour ingredients into glass. No garnish.

Mojito

Fresh lime
Fresh mint
1 tsp sugar
45 mL white rum
Dash bitters
Soda

Muddle lime, mint and sugar then add rum and bitters and top with soda.

Moscow Mule

30 mL vodka
Dash lime juice
Top with ginger beer

Build ingredients over ice. Garnish with lime wedge.

Mudslide

20 mL vodka
205 mL Kahlua
20 mL Baileys
45 mL milk
45 mL cream

Blend ingredients with ice and pour into chocolate-rimmed glass.

Orgasm

30 mL Baileys
30 mL Cointreau

Build ingredients over ice. Garnish with one or two cherries.

Penguin

15 mL black sambuca
15 mL white sambuca

Layer ingredients in order listed.

Pimm's No. 1

30 mL Pimm's No. 1
Top with ½ ginger ale
Top with ½ lemonade

Build ingredients over ice and garnish with fruit slices.

Pina Colada

30 mL white rum
30 mL Malibu
30 mL cream or coconut cream
90 mL pineapple juice

Shake ingredients with ice and strain over crushed ice. Garnish with a pineapple flag.

Pink Squirrel

30 mL crème de cacao (white)
30 mL Malibu
30 mL cream
Dash grenadine

[small]

Shake all ingredients with ice and strain. Garnish a mounted cherry and sprinkle with nutmeg.

Planters Punch

45 mL white rum
30 mL Sour Mix
60 mL orange juice
Dash Angostura Bitters
15 mL Bundaberg UP (float)
Dash grenadine

Build ingredients over ice, adding grenadine last. Garnish with orange and lime slices.

Quick Fuck

10 mL Kahlua
10 mL Midori
10 mL Baileys

Layer ingredients in order listed.

Rock Lobster

10 mL Grand Marnier
10 mL amaretto
10 mL cream (float)

Layer ingredients in order listed.

Rusty Nail

30 mL Johnnie Walker Red
15 mL Drambuie

Build ingredients over ice and garnish with lemon twist.

Sambuca Milkshake

30 mL sambuca
30 mL triple sec
60 mL milk
1 scoop ice-cream

Blend ingredients with ice. No garnish.

Screaming Orgasm

20 mL Baileys
20 mL Cointreau
20 mL Galliano
30 mL cream (float)

Build ingredients over ice. Garnish with one or two cherries.

Screwdriver

30 mL vodka
Top with orange juice

Build ingredients over ice. Garnish with orange slice.

Seabreeze

30 mL vodka
60 mL cranberry juice
60 mL grapefruit juice

Build ingredients over ice. Garnish with lime wedge.

Sex on the Beach

30 mL vodka
30 mL peach schnapps
15 mL amaretto
60 mL cranberry juice
30 mL orange juice

Build ingredients over ice. Garnish with orange slice and cherry.

Sidecar

30 mL brandy
15 mL triple sec
30 mL Sour Mix

Shake with ice and strain. Garnish with lemon twist.

[small]

Silk Panties

30 mL vodka
30 mL peach schnapps

Shake ingredients with ice and strain.

Silver Bullet

15 mL sambuca
15 mL vodka

Layer ingredients in order listed.

Singapore Sling

30 mL gin
15 mL cherry brandy
30 mL Sour Mix
Dash grenadine
Top with soda

Build all ingredients over ice. Garnish with orange slice and cherry.

Sleighride

20 mL melon liqueur
20 mL coconut liqueur
20mL Frangelico
15 mL milk
15 mL cream

Blend ingredients with ice. Garnish with cherry.

Slippery Nipple

15 mL sambuca
15 mL Baileys

Layer ingredients in order listed.

Snakebite

15 mL sambuca
15 mL Green Chartreuse

Layer ingredients in order listed.

Splice

30 mL Midori
30 mL Malibu
90 mL pineapple juice
30 mL cream (float)

Build ingredients over ice in order listed. Garnish with pineapple flower.

Spritzer

¾ white wine
¼ soda

Add ingredients to glass in order listed.

Tequila Lip Sip Suck

30 mL tequila
Lemon slice
Salt

Serve shot of tequila with lemon slice and salt shaker.

Tequila Slammer

30 mL tequila
30 mL lemonade/ginger ale

Add all ingredients in glass (no ice), cover with hand and 'slam' on bar.

Tequila Sunrise

30 mL tequila
Top with orange juice
Drop grenadine

Build ingredients over ice in order listed. Garnish with an orange slice and cherry.

Toasted Almond

30 mL amaretto
30 mL Kahlua
30 mL milk
30 mL cream

Build ingredients over ice and garnish with nutmeg sprinkles.

Toblerone

15 mL Baileys
15 mL Kahlua
15 mL Frangelico
15 mL white crème de cacao
1 tsp honey
15 mL milk
15 mL cream

Blend all ingredients with ice and pour into chocolate rimmed glass.

Tom Collins

45 mL gin
30 mL Sour Mix
Top with soda

Build ingredients over ice. Garnish with lemon slice and cherry.

West Indies Yellow Bird

30 mL white rum
15 mL banana liqueur
15 mL Galliano
60 mL pineapple juice
60 mL orange juice
30 mL Sour Mix

Shake ingredients with ice and strain over ice. Garnish with pineapple flag.

Whiskey Sour

45 mL rye whisky
60 mL Sour Mix
Egg white

Shake ingredients over ice and strain. Garnish with cherry.

White Russian

30 mL vodka
30 mL Kahlua
30 mL milk
30 mL cream

Build ingredients over ice. Garnish with cherry.

Woo Woo

30 mL vodka
30 mL peach schnapps
30 mL cranberry juice

[small]

Shake ingredients with ice and strain. Garnish with lime wedge.

Zombie

15 mL gold rum
15 mL dark rum
15 mL amaretto
30 mL pineapple juice
1 tsp passionfruit pulp
15 mL OP rum (float)

Build ingredients over ice. Garnish with pineapple flag.

Non-alcoholic cocktails

Cocktail bars should feature at least a couple of 'mocktails' (cocktails minus the kick). This provides an option for the designated driver as well as for those who may not want to have a highly alcoholic cocktail.

Mocktails can be as simple as a mixture of fresh juices or as elaborate as a Virgin Bananaberry Daiquiri. It is often up to the bartender to recommend them, as they do not sell themselves. By suggesting tasty alternatives to soft drink or juice, a bartender can often exceed customer expectations and make quite an impression.

The Monin syrup range, with more than 39 flavours in the range, makes it possible to create tantilising flavour combinations without the alcohol hit.

Lemon, Lime and Bitters

15 mL lime cordial
3–4 dashes of Angostura Bitters
Lemonade

Add Angostura Bitters around side of glass. Add ice and top with lime and lemonade.

This is a popular substitute for alcoholic drinks, although it should be noted that Angostura Bitters does have an alcohol content.

Monin Glory

15 mL Monin blueberry
15 mL Monin ginger
15 mL grapefruit juice
30 mL sparkling apple juice
15 ml lemon juice
60 mL soda water

Build ingredients over ice in order listed. Garnish with apple slice.

Peach Iced Tea

45 ml Monin peach iced tea
3–4 mint leaves
1 lime
Top water

Muddle mint and lime then add ice and top with monin peach iced tea.

Pussy Foot

60 mL orange juice
60 mL pineapple juice
Dash lemon juice
Dash grenadine

Shake ingredients with ice. Garnish with cherry.

[large]

Robo Coke

15 mL Monin melon
15 mL Monin blueberry
60 mL Coke

Build ingredients over ice. Garnish with cherry.

Shirley Temple

Lemonade
Dash grenadine

Build ingredients over ice. Garnish with orange slice.

Spiced Tomato Juice

Tomato juice
3 dashes of Worcestershire sauce
3 drops Tabasco
Salt and pepper
Dash lemon juice

Shake all ingredients with ice and strain. Garnish with celery stick

Strawberry Jaffa

30 mL Monin strawberry
30 mL Monin Swiss chocolate
90 mL orange juice
3 strawberries

Blend ingredients with ice. Garnish with strawberry fan.

Virgin Bananaberry Daiquiri

30 mL Sour Mix
60 mL pineapple juice
½ banana
4–6 strawberries
Dash grenadine

Blend ingredients with ice and garnish with strawberry fan.

Virgin Pina Colada

Pineapple juice
30 mL Monin coconut
15 mL Monin triple sec

Build ingredients over ice. Garnish with pineapple flag.

Coffee drinks

Hot drinks are generally more popular in the colder months, and are often served as a nightcap after a fine dinner. The coffee should be espresso quality and a good supply of fresh whipped cream is a must. For something different try a dash of white crème de cacao in with the cream when beating. Special coffees have always been a restaurant bar favourite and the following list features some of the most popular combinations of coffee and liquor.

Café Nero

45 mL Galliano
Hot coffee
Whipped cream

Sugar-rim glass with Galliano then flame Galliano to melt sugar. Top with coffee and cream.

Café Royale

45 mL brandy
Hot coffee
Whipped cream

Add ingredients in order listed.

Hot Nipple

15 mL Baileys
15 mL sambucca
Hot coffee
Whipped cream
Cocoa

Add sambucca and Baileys and fill with coffee. Float whipped cream and dust with cocoa.

Irish Coffee

45 mL Irish whiskey
1 tsp sugar
Hot coffee
Whipped cream
Cocoa

Add whiskey and fill with coffee. Mix in sugar to dissolve then float whipped cream with cocoa dusting.

Italian Coffee

45 mL sambucca
Hot coffee
Whipped cream
Cocoa

Add sambucca and fill with coffee. Float whipped cream and dust with cocoa.

Jamaican Coffee

45 mL Tia Maria
Hot coffee
Whipped cream
Cocoa

Add Tia Maria and fill with coffee. Float whipped cream and dust with cocoa.

Mexican Coffee

30 mL Kahlua
15 mL tequila
Hot coffee
Whipped cream
Cocoa

Add Kahlua and tequila and fill with coffee. Float whipped cream and dust with cocoa.

Bar lingo

Most establishments have some terms used in order to communicate quickly and concisely. Expressions such as 'tables away' (send the mains out) or two top (a table for two people) are common examples of lingo found in restaurants. American chains are the biggest advocates of using bar lingo as they have seen the results in the bottom line from streamlining communication.

Below is a list of some bar expressions used by bartenders around Australia and the world.

'On the fly' 'Quickly!' Used when an item is needed immediately.

'86' 'Out of stock', 86 is most often used with regard to product lines for example, if Heineken has run out a bartender might say '86 Heineken' or 'Heineken is 86ed'. It can also be used to refer to breaking down the bar. 'Let's 86 the bar.'

'Burn the well/ice' Take the ice out of the ice well and melt it in using hot water. Or to close down the service station.

'Behind you!' 'Watch out behind!' A bartender uses this term to inform someone that he or she is moving behind them and not to turn around too quickly. This is often accompanied by a touch on the back, reinforcing the original call.

'Heads!' 'Watch your head!' Used when a bartender is in danger of standing up and banging his or her head on something (like a till drawer)

'Order' Used when one staff member is passing a drink order to another. The word 'order' means 'I have a number of drinks I need made – can you make them for me'.

'Reorder' Used when the bartender in the service station either did not understand the order or wants the other staff member to rearrange the drink into call order (see Chapter 12, Multiple Drink Mixing). 'Reorder' means, 'Please tell me the drinks again (in the right order).'

'Add-on' Add-on translates as 'I would like to add on 1–2 more drinks to the order you are already making'. It is commonly used when a bartender is already in the well when another bartender/bar-back arrives. He or she calls 'add-on' to gauge if the bartender in the well can take on two more drinks.

'On the rocks' When a drink is desired on ice – usually a premium Scotch or liqueur.

'Straight up/neat' No ice, just the spirit or liqueur by itself.

'A pair' A 'pair' refers to two of an item. For example if a bartender is adding on 2 × bourbon and Cokes, he or she would say, 'Add on – bourbon and Coke a pair.'

'Plain' The term 'plain' is used to refer to a soft drink with no spirits. 'Plain' Coke means a straight Coke. This is handy when ordering a range of mixed drinks, as the word 'plain' separates it from the other drinks.

'Jumping in' This term refers is used when a bartender enters the service station assigned to another bartender. If the bartender is busy at one end of the bar, a bar-back may decide to 'jump in' to get a glass of water.

'Jumping out' Taking a break or leaving the service station for some reason. When a bartender 'jumps out' of the well, usually another bartender/bar-back will be 'jumping in'.

'In the weeds' Overrun with workload, having trouble maintaining continuous service.

A busy bar scenario

The following example combines a number of key efficiency points into a busy bar service scenario where a bartender is working at maximum productivity.

During a busy service period John uses peripheral vision while mixing a round of drinks, keeping an eye out for new customers arriving at the bar. He makes eye contact with two new customers and signals to them that he won't be too long and the customers happily begin a conversation while waiting.

While he finishes off the order at hand, John lets one of the bar-backs know that the some of the bottled beer is running out and will need restocking at their earliest convenience. He then takes the now finished drinks around his colleague – touching him on the back to let him know not to turn around too fast.

After completing and charging for the round, John moves over to the customers he has signalled to, at the same time acknowledging two new customers who have just arrived. When he reaches the first two customers, he finds that they are not together and so he looks for an indication of who is next to be served (customers often look at the person who is rightfully next). Getting no hint, he leans towards the closest customer, wipes the bar and says, 'Hi, What can I get you?'

The customer orders two vodka and tonics and a Heineken. John quickly up-sells the customer by saying 'Stoli?' While still clearing away dirty glasses from the bar-top John looks to the customer next in line and asks 'and what would you like, mate?' The second customer is a bit taken aback by being served straight after the first, but manages to order a Crown lager and a gin and tonic. 'Gordons?' John asks.

John then moves back to the service station allocated to him at the beginning of the shift, scanning the bar for any products that may be running low. He puts the dirty glasses he has collected quickly into the glasswasher and empties the ashtray.

By the time he reaches the service station he has already decided in what order he will mix the drinks. Picking up three spirit glasses with his left hand, he looks up at the bar crowd and smiles – letting his customers know that he's in control and shouldn't take too long.

John adds ice to all three glasses with one quick motion and places them onto the building tray. Picking up the vodka without looking (it's always in the same spot), he drag-pours two shots into the awaiting spirit glasses. Replacing the vodka, he grabs the Gordons off the speed rack and pours a shot into the jigger. Dunking the shot of gin in, John thinks about what's next. He sees that one of the bar assistants is at the fridge stocking the beers and calls out – 'can you grab me a Heineken and a Crown Lager, on the fly?' Using both hands, John quickly add the mixers, straws and garnishes to the drinks, turning around to see if his assistant is ready to pass him the two bottled beers.

Receiving the beers, he rushes the combined order over to the two waiting customers. While out of the service station, another bartender calls out 'jumping in', signifying that he will be using the station to prepare his drinks. John nods in acknowledgement.

John places the two completed orders in front of each respective customer, at the same time telling them how much each order costs and taking the two lots of money. Separating the notes between his fingers, he goes to the till – ringing up each order individually. Once at the till, John again looks around the bar to see if there are any other customers are waiting for service.

Seeing the customer who he acknowledged last is getting a little a anxious, he calls to his assistant to take the change back to the original customers and moves directly over to the next in line to take his order. Apologising for the wait, John greets the customer with a smile and asks for an order – clearing the bar as he goes and scanning for anything that may be starting to run low.

Index

Bold indicates recipes